What Am I Thinking?

Published by Vital Publishing. 6650 rivers ave suite 100, Charleston SC 29406

Vital is a trademark of Vital Publishing

HEALPING PEOPLE EXPERIENCE THE HEART OF GOD

Book & Ebook available wherever digital books are sold.

www.dredwardjohnson.org
facebook: @officialdrjohnson
Instagram: @drjohnsworld

Any emphases in Scripture quotations are the author's.

Some names and identifying details have been changed within the stories in this book to protect the privacy of the individuals.

ISBN: 978-7673437234

(Print)

Table of Contents

INTRODUCTION

Trying to kick a bad habit or a wrong way of thinking could be a real challenge because we tend to stick to a routine as humans. The most challenging thing to do in life is to change. We tend to operate in the same way we have been in the past for the most part.

In psychology, the longer a behavior persists, the more deeply it is established and the more difficult it is to break. This holds true for all kinds of habits, including how we think. So, to change, you must first learn to change the way you think. You are largely a product of your thought. Who you are and who you want to become start with what you think.

To become the best version of yourself and the best God wants you to be, you will have to be true to yourself. You must admit that certain things need to change in your life. The Bible says:

"That you put off, concerning your former conduct, the old man which grows corrupt according to the deceitful lusts, and be renewed in the spirit of your mind, and that you put on the new man which was created according to God, in true righteousness and holiness."

Ephesians 4:22-24

You see, there must be a shift away from your old way of life and thinking pattern. Bad habits such as using filthy language, losing control of one's anger, consuming drugs or alcohol, indulging in slander or lying, or engaging in pornography or sexual promiscuity must be eradicated. All of these takes intentionality and willingness to change first before God can help you. There must be a willingness to change first, then God empowers you by grace and makes the change you desire a reality.

It's not enough to know what has to be changed. In addition, you'll have to figure out how to create them. You see, God's word is the finest source of self-help and self-improvement instruction and inspiration that can bring the transformation you need

The fact that you are a Christian, religious, or spiritual person does not mean you have a relationship with God that could bring you transformation. Having a clear knowledge of who God is and what He says about you is the first step towards discovering your identity in Him. Find out in this power-packed transformation tool about how you can become the best version of yourself through intentionality, discipline and a consistent fellowship with God.

CHAPTER ONE:
I LIKE ME? OR DO I?

How do you learn to see the best in yourself when all you can see is your mess? How do you love yourself when you've always disliked yourself? Do you get to do yourself when you have the chance or allow what people say to discourage you from whom you are?

The truth is, your true potential can only be known by God, and He is always directing you in that direction. The best version of yourself is only in God. Anything outside of Him will be a struggle. In other words, we are God's creation, made in the same image as Christ Jesus to carry out the good works that God had planned for us to do from the beginning of time.

You are not your work; your life is not a project for you to work on. God has a plan for your life. Your creator, God, understands exactly what you were meant to be.

The Fullness of Your Life in the Spirit

In God's plan for your life, you are meant to thrive—to accept life from the outside and to create vitality inside yourself, as well as to benefit others. As a result of flourishing, you are in perfect harmony with all of these things: God, other people and the rest of creation. It is impossible to evaluate happiness by how much money you make, how much stuff you have, or how pretty you are. Becoming the unique individual God intended for you to be is the goal of this process.

A New Creation

You will change as you mature, but you will always be who you are. On the other hand, a bush rose cannot be grown from an acorn. It won't be a shrub, whether it's a robust oak or a stunted oak. Your body and intellect were meticulously created by God. God made you who you are. A common misconception is that one must transform into someone else to progress spiritually. But this is not true. God has given you the basic resource that the real you find expression in God.

Nothing is created by God just to be thrown away afterwards. The good news is this: The more you grow, the more unique you become. The person God had in mind when he created you grows. You don't simply become a better person; you grow into a better person. Yes, you grow into your own unique persona. A "new creation" is what God desires for you. Instead of exchanging you, God desires to redeem you. The person I want to become is someone I embrace as God's gift to me.

Subsequently, doing what you enjoy and what adds value are more important than how much money you make. In the face of adversity, you get stronger by the value you have developed, not by the money in your bank account. As you progress in your life, you change.

4

In the end, what more could you desire than to live out your purpose? You must understand that what God has called me to accomplish is something I desire. Therefore, God's purpose for my life will be infused into my desires.

Let Love Lead

Likewise, my capacity to love is a measure of the 'me' God designed me to be. We thrive when we are surrounded by love. That's how it works. Let love fill your heart now. When we fall in love, we are drawn into the enigma of timelessness. Because our earthly existence is only a part of the drama, nothing given in love is ever wasted. What is really important is who you become in love, not what you do.

For a growing soul, love and peace from God are essential. I am less easily disheartened if I am developing in peace inside myself. When I'm in love, I'm less likely to get upset. It was a wonderful tool for determining the state of my spiritual well-being.

Be True to Yourself

There is a person within us who has no guile or pretension. Genuine brokenness pleases God more than pretending ever could. I must be honest with myself if I am ever to become the person I want to be. Change hurts, but its required into order to be what he truly designed you to be.

Each one of us has a 'me' that we think we should be, which is at odds with the 'me' God made us be. Sometimes, letting go of that self may be a relief. Sometimes it may feel like death. I grew up needing to think of myself as a leader, as stronger, more popular, more confident than I really was. As I grew up, my need to be a leader kept me trying to be someone I wasn't. It made me more defensive, pressured, unhappy, and inauthentic. You must never let situations or certain circumstances dictate who you are. Like you and always do you at all times. Throughout this journey, you are going to learn through your will and way may not align to the path God has for you which calls for adjustments.

CHAPTER TWO:
MY JOURNEY

Stories are powerful ways to convey ideas, experiences, and instructions in a very thoughtful manner. You can use a beautiful story to inspire others and shape their lives. You can learn from the lives, mistakes and successes of others through their stories. So when you desire the same grace, ability and influence some else has, you must first learn to hear their story before you covet their glory.

Everyone has a story to tell; a culmination of our life experiences. But not all stories are interesting. Do you know why? You do not tell a story when you are passing through the motion of its experience. A story is more beautiful when you have gone through the journey of life and had emerged victoriously. This is why I will like to tell you my journey to inspire you and reset your thinking about life. I have resolved to share my journey in life, the lessons I learned, how it helped shaped me into who I am today and how my story can help you too.

THIS IS MY STORY...

My story is typical of most church Pastor's kids. I was born and raised in the Church, the faith being ever-present in my life. I grew up and accepted the Lord at the early age of 9 years when I began to work in the Church as a musician. What an amazing thing for a church boy to sing with the Choir. Later on in life, I was ordained into the office of Evangelist, a higher assignment that demands more from me. In my early twenty's, I was fully invested in the work of God, traveling locally to preach God's word to people around as God would help me. Amazingly, the Lord manifested in me through signs and wonders. All these I did while also serving my Church.

In the same manner, I excelled naturally outside the service of God. I achieved notable strides in my life when I began running a legitimate successful telecom company, which earned me multi-million dollars a year—what a huge chunk of money for a young man like me in his twenties. However, I began to lose focus and sight of what God wanted my life to represent because of the so much success I had enjoyed. I failed to watch out for the enemy and recognize the plan he had for my life.

AVOIDING THE ENEMY'S PLANS AND STRATEGY

Many people are not aware that God is not the only one who has a plan for their life. The enemy also has plans too. Your enemy, the Devil, is always at you to make sure God's intention for you will not come to pass. Sometimes, the enemy will bring what seems like success to you so that you can lose the gaze of God. Other times, he could bring abusive and destructive relationships to you just to make you lose focus. Many people fall victim to the Devil's gimmick because what he presents looks harmless on the surface. But let me tell you something about the Devil, the number one enemy of humanity.

The Devil is always subtle and deceptive in His approach. The Bible describes him as cunning. He disguises his evil plans in the most appealing ways and if you're not watchful enough, you will be caught in one of his numerous plans. The apostle Paul said;

> *"lest Satan should take advantage of us; for we are not ignorant of his devices."*
>
> **- II Corinthians 2:11**

The Devil has a few ways or plans to get you to forget your calling. He would twist what is wrong and makes it look right and use God's word to mean something else. The same deception the Devil used for Eve at the Garden of Eden is what he still uses today (Genesis 3:4). Disobedience and distraction is the devil strategic plan to take us away from God's will. Never give the Devil a chance to fulfill his plans for your life.

The Devil will fully exploit any helping hand you offer to him by falling out of God's true purpose for your life. You need to be awake to the ploys and schemes of the Devil. One way the Devil can distract you from God's plans is to keep you busy with worldly pleasures and pursuits, making you chase the clout. You could get busy with wanting to acquire wealth and fame so much that you would forget God in the process. You need to have the mindset that you will never hold on too long to things the Lord had not given to you. Martha fell prey to this plan (Luke 10:38-

42). As a believer, only one thing matters to you; every other thing is secondary.

Another Devil's plan or strategy is to deprive you of basic things that can help you live a good life. This is the plan of frustration. By taking away things that would make life easier for you or things that have some level of importance, he forces you into a corner. His plan is to get you to go against your Christian values and way of life. The ultimate aim of the Devil's plan is to cause you to sin against God. If you don't have the things you desire in life, you might be willing to go the extra mile to get them and that means taking a path that is not ordained by God.

The story of Job comes to mind in this case too. Job was a man who had everything; health, wealth, children and everything. However, the Devil wanted him to lose all so that in his need to reclaim all that he had lost, he would curse God and sin.

"Now there was a day when his sons and daughters were eating and drinking wine in their oldest brother's house; and a messenger came to Job and said, "The oxen were plowing and the donkeys feeding beside them, when the Sabeans raided them and took them away—indeed they have killed the servants with the edge of the sword; and I alone have escaped to tell you!"

- Job 1:13-15

Underestimating the plans of the Devil in your life can be very destructive. There are times when things could be challenging and you are forced to think of solutions to your problems other than going to God in prayers. Remember that the Devil is not idle. He is very aware and might be part of his plan to push you away from God. Be vigilant and take heed of this device of the Devil.

Another way the enemy plans is to give you challenges to tackle. This could range from financial concerns, anger issues, or weakness you have to struggle with always. There are little foxes that spoil the vine, which the Devil presents to us. Stay alert and choose to stay with God, regardless of whatever situation you find yourself in. Do not allow indiscipline or negligence to make you a victim of the enemy's plans.

I had to take my time to explain some of these plans of the enemy because I fell prey to some of them, even though I had a good start in my life journey. I got lost in my search for wealth. So, greed took hold of my life in the process. In fact, the enemy's choicest targets are preachers and men of God because he knows that many will go down with you if he brings you down. Make no mistake. That you're a preacher doesn't make you immune to the Devil's plans. Like most believers, including preachers, if we are not careful, we can allow carnality to grow in us. Our mindsets will change from what we used to believe to be true into something the Devil introduces to us.

Little did I know at that time that my thoughts had begun to change for the worse? As a businessman, I was graced by God with the ability to negotiate multi-million contracts with fortune 100 companies. The more deals I struck, the greedier I became to land more deals. This negative thinking opened me up to the enemy. I began cutting corners in my deals to fulfill my obligations due to the many deals I had on the table. All of this was going on while I would lay hands, cast out devils, worshiped the Lord and the Church went up in glory.

Little did I know that I was hemorrhaging, and my way of thinking was incorrect and I could not see nor feel it. I suffered spiritual blood loss while serving the Lord as a minister with unwashed hands. I never recognized or acknowledged that my thought process had changed. You see, when you begin to think wrong and expose yourself to the whims of the Devil, your belief will change, and then what you think and feel will become your new behavior.

Pride and arrogance became my friends. I was a person who grew up with nothing, but I was now able to afford whatever I liked and it became my drug. I wanted more. I wanted to land more deals, not realizing or even caring that I couldn't finalize the other deals I started. I had evolved into something that God no longer recognize. When you allow your mind to regulate your heart, flesh and spirit, you will begin to take on the behavior of that thought or feeling without knowing you are changing. I was getting lost.

Spiritually, I was still preaching, still singing and helping people with words of wisdom across the world. However, I wasn't taking my own advice like most people. It is quite easy to dole out advice but taking it is very difficult. I got married , but I did not realize that I was bringing her and making her a part of my upside-down world.

MOVING DOWNHILL

When all the deals started to implode because I was drowning in obligations, I started spiraling down by trying to keep everything afloat. Things took a turn for the worse in 2016 when I was arrested by the FBI.

The FBI immediately released a statement on why they arrested me, which was aired on many media outlets. I was later officially indicted by a federal grand jury in the summer of 2016. What they alleged me for turned out to be false, but the verdict had already been given. My life was about to be turned upside down. My life changed and things got worse.

My family moved out of our posh home into a bug-infested apartment with no lights in the bathroom and barely running water. When the news displayed my arrest, people I thought were my friends turned their backs on my wife and me, and others who were pastors and saints went online to mock my downfall. Some even added to the lies and rumors being spread about me.

For the two years that I was on pre-trial release, my family moved several times. We lost our car because the dealership saw the news and confiscated their vehicle back. I went into a deep depression because I knew my life and family would never be the same again. I had to cease working on my business due to the federal accusations and arrest. Thus, leaving my wife to work and take care of the household.

My wife had to endure going out in public, listening to people spread accusations about me, particularly to a false case. The hardest thing for me was to know that the charges against me were false, even though I knew I was not perfect in my business dealings. There was little hope for me going to trial. The government has a horrific reputation for winning 99% of its cases. I knew no matter what I did, I was going to Federal Prison.

So in those years of my pre-trial, I had to sign up for medical school to start my basic science online since I could no longer work. Scared, mad, troubled, and with several other emotions running through me, I realized that my fate and that of my family are in God's hands. I could recall an instance in while on pre-trial when I tried fighting my case and was told to appear to my probation agent.

But, little did I know they were trying to violate me and send me to jail before being sentenced. So, on the way to the federal building, I found out that the US task force was hunting me to ensure I show up to the hearing. While driving to the federal building, several pickup trucks swarmed my father's car and US marshals jumped out in full battle fatigues with assault rifles. It was just like the scenes taken out of the hit TV series "24." The experience was traumatic.

My family endured harassment, threats, and more, throughout my 2 years on pre-trial. During those times, I had to ask God with so much grief and pain in my heart; God, where are you? I know I am not perfect, but lies are being labeled against me. People have turned their backs on me. Why am I going through this? In those times, my wife told me that God said to her that He was resetting my life, and there are things that I will have to go through.

THE DILEMMA

After the pre-trial, the federal government tried to sentence me to nine (9) years in prison, but God touched the judge's heart. The sentence was reduced to four and a half (4 ½) years for one count charge. I felt hurt and angry about my life and God. I felt so alone, frustrated and depressed as I was ushered out of the courtroom to immediately start my sentence. Sadly, I left behind a wife and two small babies to fend for themselves while I went for a four and half year jail term because I opened the door of my heart to the Devil through my negative thinking and unhealthy behavior.

During those years of my incarceration who I thought was in my corner abandoned me. I was left alone to fend myself and my well being. Mental Attacks are real and when you are isolated in prison, you have nothing but your mind, which can be very dangerous. My marriage was over as she left me while in prison, and this man who preached to thousands, never received a card or letter in the mail. Now that's what you are talking about when it comes to mental attacks!

DIVINE INTERVENTION

God spoke to me and told me that this pause in my life was stamped by Him to reset my life because He still needs me and His purpose for my life is still present. For two and half years. He wanted me to change the way I thought and to become the best version of myself, the way he saw me. I was transferred to 4 federal prisons, from the camp life to the hardest prisons. Life in prison was not easy.

God allowed me to fight for my release and I spend nearly 9 months fighting for my freedom. I realized that no matter the amount of lawyers I was using to petition my freedom, I realized that only God could release me from this nightmare. All praises be to God that through petitioning and through prayer, the same judge that sentenced me to four and a half years of prison vacated the remaining portion of my sentence. Amazing! I was granted an immediate release! God had told me before the release that He would not release me unless he knew I changed. God was after my heart. He wanted a renewal, a transformation and regeneration to begin in my heart. He knows that once the heart is right, the life will be correct.

Those two and a half years changed my heart totally. It changed my thinking. I began to focus on what God wanted for my life. While in prison, I preached at all 4 institutions and thousands were collectively saved, delivered, healed and set free. I walked out of prison excepting my wrongs in life, but I vowed to God to be a new man with a new mindset. I have learned that it was my negative thinking and behavior that was the root of my issues. I would love to share with you in this book what the Lord has shared with me.

CHAPTER THREE:
YOUR NEGATIVE THINKING

"Negative thoughts stick around because we believe them, not because we want them or choose them."

- Andrew J. Bernstein

Thoughts are so powerful that it shapes your life and destiny, in fact here is what the bible has to say about thoughts; "For as he thinks in his heart, so is he" (Proverb 23:7a). The quality of your life is dependent on your thought. You are truly a product of what you think; there are no two ways about it. You can think yourself in and out of anything. You are helplessly at the mercy of your mindset, Job speaking said; "For the thing I greatly feared has come upon me, and what I dreaded has happened to me" (Job 3:25).

You thought is a voice in the realms of the Spirit. It speaks and reflects in your physical realities. Your thought is one of your biggest limitations or progress. It is responsible for your impact, growth and limitation. If you ignore your thoughts or live it to chance, then there is one sure way–failure in every respect. You can never be changed until your thinking changes. Your mindset reflects your thoughts which determines your response to God, people, Satan, situations and success.

There is something you have been thinking or have not been thinking that is responsible for where you are currently or where you want to be. Most people around us today have a mindset problem because of what they think and brood on. It doesn't matter the abundance you have physically in your hands; you will surely lose it if your mind doesn't accept it. What I mean to say is that your physical realities are directly proportional to your thinking.

Subsequently, the activities you do is a replay of our thought. Jesus gave the reason why the heathen pray the way they do; "… For they THINK that they will be heard for their many words" (Matthew 6:7). The same way you have been behaving, talking, and living in a certain manner because you THINK is how it should be. Now here is Paul's recommendation on thoughts;

"Finally, brethren, whatever things are true, whatever things are noble, whatever things are just, whatever things are pure, whatever things are lovely, whatever things are of good report, if there is any virtue and if there is anything praiseworthy – meditate on these things."

- Philippians 4:8

Everybody thinks, whether you like it or not. However, the only difference in our thinking is the direction of the thought. Thinking like God is a possibility. You can recalibrate and strengthen your thought to think like Him. You were created in His image and likeness. Therefore, you shouldn't think any lesser than your creator (God).

Just in case you have been having a mental block. Maybe you have wondered why you are still at your current level despite all you have tried to do. Also, you might feel that no reason for predicaments, miseries and down moments you are experiencing. The good news is that the tide is about to shift in your favor. Expect a transformation from your current level to where God wants you to be, your challenges, bills, health status, notwithstanding.

IT ALL STARTS AS A THOUGHT

"For the thing which I greatly feared is come upon me, and that which I was afraid of has come unto me."

- Job 3:25

According to the above scriptures, it seemed to me that Job had been dwelling on losing his wealth, children and health until it finally came upon him. Although he was the greatest man from the East in his time, he allowed fear and insecurity to occupy his mind. He spoke his fears and that became his reality.

The book of Luke 6:45 tells us the one reason why people speak the way they do. It says, "A good man out of the good treasure of his heart brings forth good; and an evil man out of the evil treasure of his heart brings forth evil. For out of the abundance of the heart his mouth speaks."

In my few years in ministry, I have met very pessimistic personalities. For years, I have wondered why it was so. These people totally do not see and speak anything good about any situation. But, when I came across the above scripture, my perspective about pessimism changed. Until you change your thought, you cannot change your life, no matter how you try.

UNDERSTANDING THE MIND

Understanding the mind is not something that even the world's best scientists, doctors, historians, or philosophers can explain. The best of their explanations are only speculations. The reason for this is that the mind is a divine entity, birthed from a spirit realm. It cannot be touched or seen.

The mind is the center of man's thinking and judgments. It holds power to imagine, recognize, appreciate, and process moods and reactions, resulting in behaviors and actions. This means you can make, remember, evaluate, and process images for meaning. That is, you can give interpret the images you get. You can also process those images for reason, language, and expression. All of these take place in the mind.

When your eyes focus on an image, it's your mind that interprets that image, and that's when you really see. If your mind can't interpret it, it doesn't matter what the image is; it'll make no sense to you. For instance, if you come across a code probably in the army and your mind has not been trained to understand it. Those codes will be meaningless to you. Your first surprise would be that although they might be numeric or alphanumeric, they will never make any sense to you. This is the power of understanding, which only can be found in mind.

In the Bible, several words were used interchangeably to refer to the mind or its activities. Examples of such words are thoughts, reasoning, imagination, thinking, and inclination. Sometimes, you'll read scripture in one Bible version where the word "thought" is used. Still, another version expresses the same word as "reasoning." You'll also find the words "mind," "soul," and "heart" being substituted for each other. But, the mind is not the heart, and the heart is not the soul. Sometimes, "soul," "heart," "the hidden man of the heart," and "spirit" is used to describe the inward man (which comprises the human spirit and his soul).

These are just generic expressions of the inward man you will find being used synonymously throughout the scriptures. And they're just a fraction of the vast number of synonyms used in expressing the phenomenon of the mind and its activities. Therefore, your mind can see, hear, perceive and interpret, even though you can't physically locate it in your body. It resides in your soul and is a spiritual entity that only God can see (Hebrews 4:12).

THE ORIGIN OF WORDS

Each word spoken is always a product of an idea - thoughts. Thoughts are seeds giving birth to words, then action. Words turn back into ideas (seeds) in people's minds. When Adam fell, the human mind was affected. It no longer took its orders from a dimension where God's Spirit dwells. Hence, the reason for spiritual and mind deadness in humanity.

When you become spiritually dead on the inside, you will begin to live according to what you perceive from your environment. That was what happened to Adam. The biggest outside influence was Satan and his demons. They fed the first generation of mankind with all kinds of thoughts. Where do you think Cain got the idea to kill his brother Abel? There had never been death or murder in the Garden. Cain didn't know what these things were! Someone had to introduce that idea and image into his mind, and that someone was Satan the destroyer.

The devil whispers thought to our mind. These thoughts are negative and they are not ours. You make them yours when you move in the direction where the thinking seems to lead you. So, you see that negative thoughts do not originate from you. It is an upshot from the devil through external enticement. However, Jesus taught us that we can either accept a thought or reject it when he said;

"Take no thought, saying...."

- Matthew 6:31

Jesus knows the enemy shoots thoughts at us. As children of God, the devil has no access to our spirits, but he can introduce thoughts to our minds. You can resist evil thoughts by speaking God's word. When negative thoughts come against you, do not be silent. You cannot overcome evil thoughts with good. Rather, you overcome evil thoughts with positive spoken words.

Your enemy, the devil, has the assignment to fill your mind with lots of negative thoughts through deception. He will use a little of God's Word and then blend it with lies just to get you off track as he did for Eve (Genesis 3:1-3). Manipulation is a strategy the devil employs to distract you from God's word.

However, Jesus gave us a way out of Satan's gimmicks. You can reject ungodly images and ideas that subtly attack your mind. The Bible says that you should cast down every evil imagination and thoughts that have exhorted itself against the knowledge of God (2 Corinthians 10:5). So, if the thought is against the knowledge of Christ, it must be pulled down.

Also, your meditation on God's word can shut down negative thinking. When you meditate, you are feeding your mind with the right food it needs to grow. Whatever the mind receives is what it processes into action and reality. So, when God's word becomes your everyday meditation, it becomes more real to you than what is happening around you.

While worrying negatively affects the mind, meditation brings peace, love, joy and assurance to a troubling mind. You just have to choose rightly—enough of worrying about what you cannot change. Let your thought process focus on what God had said. Many had not fully grasped the potential of meditation. It is a phenomenon that renews your mind.

The process of renewing or renovating your mind with God's word gives victory over negative suggestions from the devil. Rather than thinking about God's word, Adam and Eve talked to the serpent instead of speaking to God or speaking to God. When the thought that is contrary to God's word comes running through your mind, causing unease in your spirit, you must learn to quickly attack it with God's word. Stay in communion with the Holy Ghost and line up every thought with the truth of God's Word.

NEGATIVE MIND...NEGATIVE LIFE...

You can only change the quality of your life by how you think. The greatest war a man will ever fight is the battle of the mind. The devil understands this so well that he uses our mind against us. Our weapon of warfare has the power from God to destroy the enemy's strong places. This is why you cannot undermine the potency of God's word because it is your weapon to victory. We capture every thought and make it give up and obey Christ through the declaration of God's marvelous council.

God is the source of sound ideas. They originate from the spiritual realm. In the beginning, there was only one source of ideas, who is God. Now, the devil had made a counterfeit of what God created, which has brought chaos to our word.

The Bible says,

"For my thoughts are not your thoughts, neither are your ways my ways, says the LORD."

- Isaiah 55:8

Awesome! God is talking about the quality of His ideas. He says the kind of ideas from Him is better and more powerful than any other one. If truly ideas rule the world, then the better your ideas' quality, the more dominion you have on earth. The Scriptures says, "But we have the mind of Christ."(1 Corinthians 2:6). You have a mind that can think the same way God thinks - this is unique!

Unlike our natural mind, which only thinks of lack, impossibilities and limitations, our renewed minds can think miracles. But the negative thinking of many people has kept them in their current state. A negative mind automatically transforms into a negative life. Avoid negativity. The truth is, negative thoughts will come. But when it comes, you should not only resist it learn to replace it with some positivity through God's word.

CHAPTER FOUR:
RESETTING YOUR MIND

"Progress is impossible without change, and those who cannot change their minds cannot change anything."

- George Bernard Shaw

If you want to change how you think, then change what you exposed your mind to. The mind is one of the most powerful elements of mankind that can change and shape your life. Any attack or progress in life starts in mind. Nothing happens in you or through you without passing the gateway of the mind.

Are you tired of the repeated failure? Do you want a shift in your life? Do you desire to change your life, relationship, family, or profession? You need not look too far. What needs to change is right there in you the mind. If you want to change your situation and hope for a better life, the first step is to reset your mind.

THE POWER OF THE MIND

We all grow up individually within a society that affects the way we think. The people around your environment have a lot of influence on your mind. Their way of life affects your perspective about life because you have grown to understand your mind's unconscious condition. So, if your society presents evil to you as good, you will not choose to see that evil acts as a sign of goodness. The conditioning of your mind is such that you begin to think, act and live by what you have seen others in your community do and imitate.

The mind is the seat of thoughts and actions. This simply means that your behaviors are controlled by the things that you think about constantly. Some people believe that they are not in control of what comes in and out of their minds every day a way to justify the negativity and terrible thoughts that they entertain. The truth is, you are in control of what comes into your mind. You are in control of what you feed on. Now, if you believe otherwise, the process of resetting your mind and changing the way you think is near impossible because that is where you ideally will start from.

The mind's power is available to all and sundry and we wield it whether or not we like it. If you have not realized that you hold this power, chances are that you are not wielding it effectively and you have allowed a lot of negatives to seep through it. But, when you are aware you hold such a special power of the mind to change life situations and yourself, you will ensure that you put every structure in place to give your thoughts precision and direction.

THE 'HOW' AND 'WHAT' TO THINK

The simple principle of how the mind works is that what you think defines what you are. Since the mind controls what you think, you will be careful about how you think and think. To change what you think, you have to reset your mind and teach it to think rightly. Many people do not know how or what to think.

The ability to think is not known by everyone. Sometimes, we tend to assume thinking to be anything our mind picks randomly. But this is not true. The right-thinking process is not random. It is a well-defined stream of thoughts that follows a definite pattern about something you hope for or what to get.

Little wonder you do not attract what you desire most times because your thoughts contradict those desires. In learning how to think right, you must use your words correctly. Always be positive about what you will do and you will see yourself thinking about how it can be done. For example, do not say, "I cannot do this." Rather, say, "I will try and do it." It is in trying you will think on the possible ways by which it could be done.

"Finally, brethren, whatever things are true, whatever things are noble, whatever things are just, whatever things are pure, whatever things are lovely, whatever things are of good report, if there is any virtue and if there is anything praiseworthy — meditate on these things."

- Philippians 4:8-9

Amazingly, the Bible defined what to think. Therefore, you need to start your mind reset with these things. The ultimate is that you must feed your mind on positivity to think all the time positively. The resetting of your mind begins with a transformation in your thought. The bible clearly states that a transformed mind does not conform to the world's will (Romans 12:2). The transformed mind only believes what God's word says and thinks on what it says it should.

Suppose you're unhappy with the situation you find yourself in. In that case, the chances are that you have been negligent about the power of changing your life with your mind. What you cannot change is a product of what has not changed in your mind. A dangerous habit is an upshot of the unbridled mind.

Letting your mind roam free, dwelling on negatives and feeding off it over time could affect your mind so much that all you see is negativity and impossibilities. This is why you need to reset your mind to bring forth your best. You must then teach your mind to dwell on the right things to attain what you desire. Teaching your mind to dwell on the things you desire is the new habit you must cultivate. It involves you taking control of your mind and acknowledging its power. But first, you must reset your mind.

RESETTING YOUR MIND; what does it mean?

"If you are not satisfied with what is coming to you, start to work and change your mental attitude and mental states, and you will see a change gradually setting in."

–William Walker Atkinson

If you ever consider resetting your mind, it means you have done two important things. First, you have been able to identify that your mind has the potential of affecting your life and you must put it to proper use. The second reason you would like to reset your mind is that you have made some thinking errors that you are not satisfied with and want a change.

Your actions in the past are a result of our thinking. Some of these actions had led to regret and you are now careful not to take similar action again. Therefore, learning to reset your thinking is a critical way to avoid another future regret.

Every future starts today. Since you cannot change what had happened in your past, I believe you can change what will happen in your future by what you give yourself to today. This is another opportunity for you to recreate the future you have always dream of. I want to urge you not to miss the chance, which is a process that begins in your mind.

Your mind is like a field for plantation. Whatever you plant on that field is what you will reap. However, the quality of your harvest depends on the nourishment you give to the field. There are ways you can nourish your mind to provide you with the best stuff you desire. One of these ways is to give your eyes to seeing beauty and excellence at all times. The eyes and eyes are gateways to the mind. What caused a fault in your mind came as a result of what you heard and watch.

In the same manner, the resetting process will follow a similar way. You need to give more attention to what will stretch your mind to do more. The greater exploit's motivation is an inner drive that stirs you up when you see the extent of the result others produce. If you have been producing a result of 10 on a scale of 0-100, when you see someone in the same field as yours producing a result of 99, you will feel motivated to try more. This is how your eyes' exposure to see excellence and beauty helps your mind see its possibility too in your life.

This is not your best self yet. More still left undone, especially when you see people not up to your level producing results that had become a world phenomenon. See what others are doing well, which you wish to do and let your mind dwell on their level of excellence. You are conditioning your mind for excellence when you decide to only watch and listen to people who produce excellent results. Gradually, you will begin to see changes and in no long time, you will also produce the same level of result.

THE TREASURE OF YOUR MIND

In resetting your mind, you must place value on it. When you value your mind, you will be able to recognize the wrong and terrible things you have established in it and only then can you weed them out. Fear, confusion, doubt, anxiety, worry, and all forms of negativity are issues that had become regular thoughts in most of our minds. Allowing these thoughts to into your mind means you are comfortable with the way your life is. But those who want to change their life know that comfort is a dangerous place to be for the process of transformation.

You need to become very uncomfortable sitting with negative people so that their negativity does not rub on your mind. Think positively. Speak positively and meditate on God's word. Instead of worrying, meditate. Instead of allowing confusion to dominate your heart, pray. Rather than walking in fear, step out in faith. What you are doing through this change process is conditioning your mind for a proper reset.

Make no mistake about this; negative thoughts will seek to creep in even after you have decided to get rid of them. As long as you live in this world, the devil will ensure that you know the fears, doubts and confusion that riddle this world. A troubled mind focuses on these and feeds on them.

The truth is, a reset does not mean you are unaware of these challenges. You are aware, but you take these negatives and subject them to God's will by His word. Awesome! It is good you know what God word says for any and every situation. In this way, you will know how to tackle any attack on your mind.

ACTIVATING A RESET IN YOUR MIND

"To put off your old self, this belongs to your former manner of life and is corrupt through deceitful desires, and to be renewed in the spirit of your minds, and to put on the new self, created after the likeness of God in true righteousness and holiness."

- Ephesians 4:22-24

Activating a reset in your life is to put away your old habits or destructive way of life to learn how to start all over again, this time in a very beautiful way. So, to reset your mind is to discard harmful thought patterns that affect your actions and leads to dangerous habits. This will bring you back to a place where you are ready to move unto greater works through better ways of thinking. To effect change in the way you think and change your life for the better, you need to carry out this reset. Without reset, change is impossible.

The effects of a change in mindset are exponential. You can see this in the life of Apostle Paul. His story depicts the wonderful capabilities of a mind that has been reset and renewed. Apostle Paul, formerly known as Saul, was an apostle of Jesus Christ in his days. Paul was a Pharisee with firm beliefs and convictions. In so many ways, he had sown seeds in his minds and they had taken roots, which had made him fanatical about what he believed to be true and right.

Apostle Paul believed in non-biblical traditions as firmly as he believed in the written words of the bible, though with the wrong perspective. He was a devout Pharisee and Jew. These beliefs formed the basis for his persecution against the Christians, which sometimes were violent, as was seen in the stoning of Stephen (Acts 7:54-60). Saul saw the teachings of a new messiah as false and dangerous. He refused to agree with the apostolic teachings that Jesus was the messiah.

Although Saul, who became Apostle Paul, was a religious man who believed in the Bible's teachings, his mind still withheld some wrong teachings of the Bible that compel him to take certain actions against Christians. That was Paul's life until he encountered Jesus and was taught the right teaching of the Bible. That encounter turns around Saul's life forever.

The truth is, not everyone will have the kind of encounter Paul had before they would experience a change of mind. But, when your life is not a blessing to humanity, then you should know that something had gone wrong in your mind. At those times, do not seek to change your actions. Change your mindset. What are the wrong beliefs that had eaten deep into you? How was it affecting the progress and growth of the human race? What can you do to change? These questions will birth a new you.

THE TRAINING YOUR MIND NEEDS

"We cannot solve our problems with the same thinking we used to create them."

- Albert Einstein

The mind can be trained to recognize patterns, create routines, maintain habits, and establish limits. This can be done consciously or subconsciously (if you don't pay attention to what goes into the mind). However, the beautiful thing about the mind is the elasticity that enables it to be reset and remove patterns that are not useful. Every thought you let in shapes your mind and the brain in particular.

Resetting your mind is an acknowledgment that the current way of thinking does not favor a progressive life. It implies your actions due to your thoughts are not helping you achieve the things you desire and you're not getting the best from life. Therefore, you want to change your thought to change the result your life produces. When you seek to change a life pattern or break the limits around your life, you will need to think differently.

*"You cannot expect to live a positive life if you
hang with negative people."*

- Joel Osteen

The people around you matter a lot about your mind. You are a larger expression of the most people you live with or talk with often. If you realize that your company of friends is the reason for the limitation in your mind, change that circle of friends. How do you expect to see a positive result in your life when most of your friends are a naysayer. The mind is like a computer. It is what you give to it that it processes out. If your mind often receives negative words, you should not expect your life to produce a positive result.

Take a good lesson from Elisha's life, when his life was about to change with a double portion of Elijah's anointing. The Bible says,

*"Now the sons of the prophets who were at Bethel came out to
Elisha, and said to him, "Do you know that the LORD will take
away your master from over you today?"
And he said, "Yes, I know; keep silent!"*

- 2 Kings 2:3

Awesome! I loved Elisha's response when the sons of the prophet tried speaking negativity to his heart. He simply silences them.

The truth is, if you do not learn to silent some negative voice around you, it will come to a time when you can't resist the effect on your life. Sometimes, your mind's reset has to do with controlling what comes into your heart from your environment.

A reset offers you a fresh start from all negativity surrounding your mind. However, brewing positivity and staying positive is challenging. But, a reset makes it easier. To achieve more, you have to remove the negativities, encourage positive choices and attitudes. This is where a change in thinking begins. But then, how can you achieve this reset? I will like to share three (3) major ways to reset your mind for a better life.

Write Down Your Thoughts

To effect changes, you must first need to see what you need to change in words. This means that the mind believes what the eyes see. Get to write those limiting and negative thoughts you think had held you down. As a replacement, write the alternative positive thought you need and cancel out that negative mindset.

Those simple actions are messages to your brain to delete what you don't want and accept the new things you want. Replace as many negatives as possible with positive thoughts, dreams and ambitions. Keep track of this list and ensure that you strive to achieve what is written down.

What writing helps you achieve is to motivate you towards what had been written. Write your goals in a book and read them out loud to yourself as often as you can. That is the conditioning your mind starting in process.

Consciously Avoid and Delete Negative Sources

The thoughts you are aiming to rid yourself off has a source. To discard such thought, you must first find the source. This source can be a person, an environment, or a situation you find yourself in.

Most times, other people project their fears and negative ideas into you and your mind. Being a constant recipient of those ideas begins to process them into your life. You cannot affect any true change without cutting off the supply of such unwanted thoughts.

If the source is a person with whom you have a close relationship, it can be tricky. However, you might do away with that source by avoiding conversation and situations that build up to negatives or if you can afford to avoid such a person for some time. Transparency can also be helpful in such a situation. Explain to this person what is happening. Trying to find a way to do away with the negativity that flows from them is essential to reset your mind.

Do Not Internalize Other People's Problem

The environment and those around you have a way of affecting your mind. Finding yourself in a place of struggles and gloom where everyone seems to be battling with one serious problem or the other can affect the state of your mind. To reset your mind and free it from this, you must show empathy without internalizing the problems and negativity all around you.

When you empathize with others' worries and problems, you must be careful not to internalize those worries as yours. Isolate your thoughts from such negative thoughts. Offer advice and encouragements to those who need it and show love. But, never receive those fears and worries as yours. A reset is not possible if you go-ahead to do that.

CHAPTER FIVE:
COMMON THINKING ERRORS

"And do not be conformed to this world, but be transformed by the renewing of your mind, that may prove what is that good and acceptable and perfect will of God."

- Romans 12:2

Thinking, as a thought process, is passive reasoning influenced by internal or external factors. Your environment gives shape and structure to your thinking, which in turn affects the way you behave. Thinking is an innate nature in mankind because we have a soul, which constitutes our will and emotions. While humans have a mind for thinking, animals only have instinct because they do not have souls. Therefore, the supremacy of mankind over all other creatures is evident in the way we can utilize our environment to our advantage.

"And they said, "Come, let us build ourselves a city, and a tower whose top is in the heavens; let us make a name for ourselves, lest we be scattered abroad over the face of the whole earth.
But the LORD came down to see the city and the tower which the sons of men had built."

-Genesis 11:4-5

Whatever you can think in your mind can be in your hands. Literally, anything the mind conceives in the thought realm is possible. God acknowledged the potency of thoughts when the Babylonians tried to build a tower that would get to heaven, according to Genesis 11:4-7. While the thought was still in their mind, God saw the possibility and He said;

"Indeed the people are one and they all have one language, and this is what they begin to do; now nothing that they propose to do will be withheld from them."

- Genesis 11:6-7

Now, you could see that the whole idea of building a tower was just a proposal in the mind of the Babylonians, but God saw it as a reality. Dear reader, your thinking is action in an unseen realm. You cannot afford to think amiss. Right thinking produces real results just the same way a wrong mindset produces error.

A lot of thinking errors have been adopted as a norm in society. People are quick to pick a certain thought pattern within any society they find themselves in. These errors most often affect the people within a community. Still, they become inherited errors passed from one generation to the next. So, if a wrong thought pattern becomes a norm and is not corrected, the next generation becomes a victim of such error. This is why I have written this book by the Holy Ghost's inspiration to reset every wrong thinking pattern for a better tomorrow and beautiful future of the next generation.

There is a way how or what you think affects you and the people around you. Psychologist believes that humans are made up of different kind of thinkers. Some of these thinkers have;

✓ The ability to influence the behavior of others.

✓ The aptitude of competence to do a certain kind of work at a certain level.

✓ The attitude, either mental or emotional that characterizes a person.

✓ The behavior to which one acts in a certain way in different situations.

✓ The mental image of how a person pictures the world generally and so on.

Subsequently, your thinking is imperative and important to how you live, act, and react to situations and people around you. However, as believers, we must understand that our thinking must not conform to the world system. We have a principle that guides our thought patterns and judgment about situations, things and people. These principles are boldly written in the Bible as God's word. The misconception had always been that the Bible is God's word and everything it says we must do. But let me burst your bubbles. The Bible is not God's word. It only contains God's word and in it, you will find God's way for living and God's principles for thinking.

However, it is shameful that despite this available manual (God's word) for right thinking and living, many believers still fall victim to common thinking errors. This is why they become frustrated out of unanswered prayer. They do not understand how the principles of God's word work and how it can be rightly adopted into their thinking pattern to become a way of life that produces the desired results.

What you do not know as wrong would become a norm that anybody coming after you would take up as a lifestyle. This means a recurring of unpleasant events could continue among a family or community if the issue is not treated from its root. Most times, the devil is not in charge of our problem. We sometimes caused some of these problems for ourselves due to the fault in our thinking pattern. Hence, a need for reset in thinking is required.

To reset the way you think, you have to do away with the common thinking errors of life and to do so, you must be able to identify them. In this chapter, I will like to show you fourteen (14) thinking errors that need your urgent attention and I will proffer solution to all by God's grace. These fourteen common thinking errors include:

1. Absolute thinking: Thinking in an extreme or over-generalized way

"There is no absolute right or wrong, good or evil, but there are good manners and common decency."

- K.J. Parker

Absolute thinking is the definite conclusion to what you assume of a particular thing, idea, concept, place, or person. It is an ideology that makes you assume a thing to be totally right or wrong. Absolute think is a one-way mindset. You have no two thoughts about something you assumed. There is nothing you are ready to change for whatever assumption you have.

You believe it and that's the final, no room for adjustment or taking it off the table. It is being rigid with what you know and think. But surprisingly, this is a common thinking error. A lot of us find it hard to change our concept about a thing. These kinds of people are not flexible enough to make a lapse in what they think.

An extreme or over-generalized way of thinking comes with restrictions and limitations. It ties you down to what every other person thinks about a particular thing, issue or situation. A person with an extreme thinking pattern has little or no opinions to contribute to an ongoing discussion. They are always in the 'yes' party to what all other people agree on or the 'no' party to what all other persons are against.

The error in this type of thinking is that you have no thoughts of yourself, except the generally accepted opinion of other people's ideology. So, even when you have a new idea, your thinking would limit such an idea and shut you out of thinking creatively. The thoughts they accept are people's general thoughts, so even when you have a new thought or idea, you have to keep shut.

You must know that nobody has any power over your thoughts. Therefore, do not feel intimidated to air what you think and feel. Speak what you know to learn what you still need to know. You might not know you have not known if you do not give your chance the freedom of expression.

Consider the story of the adulterous woman, who was caught in the very act of adultery (John 8:1-10). The men who accused her brought her to Jesus so that the messiah can approve of their error in thinking. They were extremists who believed anybody caught in adultery should be stoned to death. Alas! Jesus taught them a different school of thought when he said;

"He that is without sin among you let him first cast a stone at her."

- John 8:7

Jesus wasn't in their general school of thought to killing as a substitute for a sinful act. As much as God hates sin, He does not hate His creature. So, Jesus came to show the people the love dimension of God rather than having an extreme assumption about who God is not. As Christians, we should emulate Jesus, who sees things in more than a way. Jesus learned to see the good in the most difficult situation. This is a mindset he wants us to develop daily. Making excuses for not doing something

2. I can't: MAKING EXCUSES FOR NOT DOING SOMEHTING

"I can do all things through Christ who strengthens me."

- Philippians 4:13

Any limitation of mankind is outside Christ. A person in Christ has numerous possibilities. This is the advantage of the believer, but ignorance had robbed us of what is rightfully ours. When you think it can't be done because nobody did it, you are making a big error in your think. There is nothing impossible with God, but the limitation in our mind made us think lesser than God's capacity. It is time to rise up and operate in the fullness of God's mind. Dwelling inside of you is God's Spirit. If nothing could limit God, no situation or circumstances should be impossible for you.

Truthfully, the word "I can't" is a lazy man language adopted to look like a befitting excuse for not maximizing your potential. Some people believe so much in this word of discouragement that they feel reluctant to do more with their lives and time. In fact, all they do would just seem like nothing worthy because they have sunk deep to accepting that it can't be done.

Jeremiah was a prophet who had this limiting thinking error when God called him. Jeremiah said;

"Ah, Lord God! Behold! I cannot speak, for I am a youth."

- Jeremiah 1:6

Read the former and latter verses of this Bible chapter. You'll see that Jeremiah was not so different from the people who belittle God's deposit in them due to an error in their thought pattern. Jeremiah wasn't ready to live out his full potential. He was just complacent about his current status and he wouldn't like anything more to disrupt his present comfort. When you are comfortable with where you are and what you have, complacency will limit you not to strive for more.

Now is time to break off from this limiting thinking of "I can't," "it's impossible," and "it can't be done." Avoid this negative thinking error and always aspire for something more. I will rather try a thing and fail than not try at all. This is the mindset of achievers. They are always optimistic and positive.

"Ninety-nine percent of the failures come from people who have the habit of making excuses."

- George Washington Carver

Humans are straws of excuses. We make excuses for almost everything happening or not happening in our lives. We use excuses as an attempt to cover up our lack of abilities and potentials. Most times, we excuse ourselves out of what could have taken us to the next level of our lives.

People who make excuses never make an impact. Take full responsibility for your life and do not leave your life to chances. You will reset nothing about your life if you keep making excuses to bail yourself out of what you ought to do.

It is time to make changes. Stop the excuses. Do not allow fear, self-doubt and laziness to become an excuse for you not doing what will bring joy and fulfillment to your life.

3. Rhetorical Questions: Hiding negative thoughts with questions

One secret about rhetoric questions is that it makes you indecisive because you seek answers where there is none. This could make you utterly confused or mesmerized. Indecision is destructive to change. You will be left on the fence on what your options and actions should be.

Questions like Can I? Do I? Should I? Is this it? How sure is this? And so many other rhetoric questions should stop if you truly want a reset in your thinking. Always know that where there is a will, there is a way. Once you have the will for change, go make the changes.

Stop asking questions that would damp your spirit and makes it look like nothing can change around and about your life. You have a question about life, a process, a concept, then that's okay. Ask someone who can put you through and let them see you through.

4. Awfulizing: Thinking only bad things will happen

When you keep seeing everything as bad, evil, wrong, and awful, you are in the thinking error of awfulizing. Even in a bad situation, there is an iota of goodness. That is why my encouragement to you is to always see the good in a bad situation. If you tag almost everything as bad, what or who is left in the world?

"But Peter said, "Not so Lord! For I have never eaten anything common or unclean. And a voice spoke to him again the second time, what God has cleansed you must not call common."

- Act 10:14-15

The world still has more greatness to offer. Think through the goodness of life and work with it. Not all things are bad. When others see no good in something or someone, be the one to think out how it won't be presented as awful. Take that stance and make no conclusion until it is certain.

Pessimists see no good in anyone or anything, only negatives and the possibility of wrong things dominating their minds. People like this rarely harbor strong will and positive vibes in their hearts. Even when they do, it's not for a long cause because they would see the greater negative impact or outcome sooner or later. They have nothing to be optimistic about.

People should get as much positivity into their thinking because positivity comes in handy, which you will need when things get tough or might go wrong. The truth is, good things happen too. Salvation is one of the good things that happen in our world. God has baggage full of good promises to us all who truly and divinely follow him.

So, the world is not as bad as you think. Try seeing things in a positive light and you would see how your positive thinking alone illuminates the world.

5. Statement of "fact.": Making Assumptions without knowing all the facts

Making assumptions without full knowledge of the facts is another common error in thinking. For instance, I want you to consider statements like, "He said, she said, they said, it said..." What about what you say? How about the actual fact that confirms what is being said? Have you ever stopped to think that taking what others say hook, line and sinker affects the way you think and act? Or do you just act on what people tell you?

You cannot assume to walk in a certain thinking pattern when it indicates someone's unconfirmed philosophy. When the source of information is in oblivion and the thought isn't in coherence with your principles, it is advisable not to vocalize such thoughts. Only speak what you know and what works for you. Find the fact and talk about the truth, not what someone else says is the truth.

"And you shall know the truth, and the truth shall make you free."

- John 8:32

You see, rumor and hearsay do not set people free. It is the truth. Always go for the truth. Your freedom is in the ability to find out the truth and make it your conviction for every word you say.

10. He, She, it Statements: Thinking that other people, events, or things outside of you cause you to feel a certain way

Holding others responsible for how you feel is highly unacceptable. You're responsible for yourself, not your father or mother, nor your siblings, not anyone.

How you feel, think, do and act is all you and nobody else. People may say or do things to influence your thinking pattern. Still, you are responsible for filtering what you allow into your mind. Nobody knows you better than yourself, so everything that you shouldn't take in, do well to avoid it.

You cannot keep thinking your life is turning the way others what it to be. Do not put your life or future at the mercy of someone else. Yes, I know you cannot control the external factors that make up life, but you can control the internal factors that make up your own life.

When life happens, think of ways to get out and be your own person with a free thought process and not blame people. Although people might orchestrate the problem, the solution is for you to figure it out. Reset the angle at which you bring your thoughts and think again.

6. Blaming- finding fault in other people or things

The blame game is a trick the Devil plays on us so well, and it is evident from the beginning of time at the Garden of Eden. In Genesis 3, when God questioned Adam why he ate the forbidden fruit, Adam shifted the fault to Eve and Eve shifted it to the serpent.

Let's be sincere to ourselves. Both Adam and Eve were solely responsible for what they brought upon themselves. While their thinking (knowledge) was being influenced, they had every right to say no and stop the serpent. But their interest in the serpent's offer made the serpent control their thought process.

Most times, what you need to do is accept your fault. You're guilty, you are wrong and you have to be sorry. That's all it takes to set things right. Not pointing to various people, involving them in your mistakes. Make your mind ready to be fully responsible for whatever is to come, you're on your own and your decisions make you.

7. Loaded words-Using offensive words that are disrespectful

"A good man out of the good treasure of his heart brings forth good; and an evil man out of the evil treasure of his heart brings forth evil. For out of the abundance of the heart his mouth speaks."

- Luke 6: 45

At salvation, God saved your spirit, but your soul is being saved. This means that your soul is still in the process of transition from what it used to be to what salvation has brought to it. So, you need to continuously give yourself wholly to God in prayers and the study of God's word for your soul to be whole.

Sometimes, I wonder why we have Christians who still behave irrationally. Don't they know Christ? Of course, they do. But, the way of Christ is not yet in them. They disregard people and show no respect for elders. For such people, we hide our faces in

52

contempt. Until you have allowed God's word to transform your soul, you are yet to be like Him. Let God's word teach you what to say to people

Words pierce through the heart. It kills faster than a weapon. You see, we are not only murderers when we kill someone with a weapon or bare fist. A murderer is also someone who can't tame his or her tongue but speaks carelessly to people.

You'd be surprised to know that 80% of people out there are structured by the words that are said to them and it structures them in only two ways; positively or negatively. Do you know why the world is full of broken people here and there? The reason is the words people utter daily into other people's life the lives of others. Negative and offensive words do no good to the heart of man. Instead of building up, it destroys.

8. Statements of 'Should,' demanding the world to be a certain way

The world is the way it is because humans have used their very own hands to cause massive destruction to what God has originally designed. So, when you sit down in your comfort zone and start mapping out what should be and what shouldn't be without activeness to work towards what you think, you make no difference to the evil men who contributed to the world's menace.

You're the first step to building the world right and it all starts in your mind. Your thoughts are the sole foundation of what is to be, so use it well and quit the "should-game." Precisely, the world is what you make of it and to every visualized thought you make on what ought to be, you're a step better.

Let your mind and heart stay filtered from dirty and unholy thoughts because to have God reside in you, you have to let His place of abode stay clean and filtered.

9. Sentimentality: Self serving acts

Sentimentality involves justifying your action by emphasizing the good and positive things you have done rather than considering the wrong action of the moment. A sentimental person will always lookout for ways to feel less guilty about a crime. A sentimental person would want to reduce guilt by being good to a stranger, enjoying immunity from family background, or religious pardon of God's forgiveness. The truth is, God indeed forgives, but it is an error in thinking to always assume God will forgive a wrong even when you persist in it. Even though God forgives, there is punishment and consequences for any wrongdoing.

The sentimental person allows emotions to control his or her thoughts, words, actions, and decisions. When you overindulge your thoughts, especially towards another or things, these thoughts generate some emotions. Often, these emotions become so powerful that it gets in the way of your ability to think logically and or become realistic. Sentimental thinking pattern shifts your attention from what God had done for you towards what you desire because of greed.

Consequently, a sentimental person is limited by emotions. Sentimentality is a criminal thinking error. Research has shown that most of the world's dictators were sentimental. World War two dictator Benito Mussolini and Hitler were sentimentalists. In one of His statements, Benito said that most of Hitler's commanders, who committed grave crimes and murders, usually broke down in tears in the evenings while listening to their daughters play the piano. If they were this soft, what then made them so ruthless and heartless during the day?

These men had a strong emotional attachment to events and thoughts so much that their thinking covers reality and their thoughts become their reality. Sentimentality is a way of denying reality. Even though sentimentality can be a defense mechanism against painful emotions such as anger, grief, and shame, it eventually leads to crime. This is against the instruction we find in the word of God.

"For we walk by faith, not by sight."

- 2 Corinthians 5:7

According to the above Bible text, the word 'sight' means perception the sense of sight, smell, touch, taste, and hearing. All these are triggers to our emotions. Anyone who allows themselves to be controlled by these emotional triggers robs themselves of the blessings of a peaceful and sound mind (II Timothy 1:7).

Do not allow your emotions to rule you. Rather, walk by faith in the knowledge of God's word. We live by faith. We have our being by faith. Every experience of the believer is hinged on the reality of faith. The substance of things hoped for and the evidence of things yet to be seen.

10. Grandiosity: Being impressive and imposing in appearance and style

"Casting down imaginations, and every high thing that exalts itself against the knowledge of God, and bringing into captivity every thought to the obedience of Christ."

- 2 Corinthians 10:5

In Paul's epistles, the Apostle repeatedly warned believers to avoid this singular thinking disorder. This is because of the numerous negative impacts a negative thought has, not only on you but also on others around him. Grandiosity is a thought pattern whereby a person thinks of being better than others when he or she is not, in the real sense. It is an unrealistic sense of superiority often characterized by a long-term view of being better than others.

This is a severe case and is usually not readily accepted by the person involved. The set of people with a Grandiosity mentality often feel that only a few persons can understand them. Also, they believe that the set of abilities and traits they possess are only given to a few privileged people. Some of the traits include beauty, intelligence, possessions, and so on. This thinking error breeds a sense of disdain for others. It makes you consider them as being inferior to you in every way possible.

The Lord himself resists the proud, high-minded, and grandiose. Rather than think of yourself as better than others, you should consider others better than you and think yourself lower than others. This is not in any way suggesting that you become a slave to other people. But an excessive way of disdain for other people or their ways is wrong and not such behavior that the child of God wants to exhibit.

CHAPTER SIX:
CRIMINAL THINKING AND
BEHAVIOR

How does a crime happen? Does it begin as a thought or an action? How do people feel after a crime? This chapter attempts to look into how certain thinking patterns could lead to criminal behaviors. Most times, people fall victim to a crime due to accumulated criminal thought patterns that eventually led to the criminal act. I am sure that you know that everything, action innovations, inventions, and even criminal acts originate from thoughts in the mind. Criminal thinking leads to criminal behavior and criminal act.

But then, what is Criminal thinking?

Criminal thinking is a distortion in a person's thinking pattern, which causes a thinking error that could make the person commit a criminal act. The truth is, this form of thinking error does not happen by accident. It is an accumulation of thinking error over time, which the individual ignores and later develops into a toxic behavior.

People who exhibit criminal thinking do not have to look like a criminal. But, their thought is already full of evil agenda waiting for execution. Sometimes, I wonder what could make a believer, who loves the Lord, work as a steward and minister to God's now suddenly become harden at heart. You see, criminal thinking is subtle. When you ignore the warning in your conscience, anytime your heart wanders into an evil thought, you begin to accumulate criminal thoughts. Such a person would eventually exhibit the thought through your actions.

In this chapter, I will like to share with you seven (7) essential criminal thinking and behavior you must pay attention to when you begin to see its manifestation in your thought. It is best to attack criminal thinking at the thought level before it eventually becomes a behavior that could not be curtailed until it executes the act.

1. Mollification

People who have a mollification thinking error always make excuses for the crime they commit. They blame their criminal behavior on some sort of externality and justify their action just to avoid being responsible for their wrongdoing.

This kind of thinking makes a person have a perceive injustice about life. Therefore, they always try to prove to themselves and others that the crime they commit happened because they had no choice. You see, people who do not take responsibility for their actions will never see reasons to change. This makes it complex for people with this kind of thinking disorder to actually change. Hence, they keep living the criminal lifestyle.

However, anyone who desires to be free from such thought patterns or behavior must first take responsibility for their action. They must stop to justify any criminal act they commit. Also, I have shown you from my story in the first chapter of this book that it must begin with you if you will ever change anything in your life. Never blame any externality about the challenges in your life. Take responsibility for your life.

2. Cut off

The Cut off mentality is often similar to mollification. It ignores the sense of responsibility for any wrong action. However, a cut-off thinking pattern implies being committed to a criminal lifestyle by indulging in an act that fuels and increases the tendency to commit the crime more. For example, some people take drugs, alcohol, or heroin as a cut-off before carrying out a criminal act. Cut off shut you off from rational human thinking to damn the consequence for any action you take.

Nevertheless, people can correct the cut-off thinking error by creating a replacement in their thoughts. Most times, someone addicted to a drug might not easily let go of it. But finding a substitute like a particular food each time such urge for the drug will help eliminate the cut-off. Also, it is advisable to always stop, think and consider the consequences of your action before taking a step. My best advice to anyone with a cut-off behavior is to get busy. Develop a skill or craft that would help you focus on building a good life for yourself and your family.

3. Entitlement

You see, people do not just commit crimes without first convincing themselves through their thought that they have the permission to commit the crime. It occurs when you begin to give yourself reasons why you should commit the crime. For instance, someone who had a rough past, hurt from a previous relationship, or gets disappointed and begins to feel entitled to commit a crime is an error in the person's thinking faculty.

Entitlement thinking makes you feel you are above the law. Therefore, whatever criminal thought that floods your mind becomes justifiable. A person with criminal entitlement thinking can be so manipulative. Such an individual could often use a divide and rule approach to create conflict between people, usually in a relationship or workplace, just to commit a crime and make it look like the crime is justifiable.

Consequently, anyone with an entitlement thinking pattern always has this sense of ownership for everything. They often misrepresent wants for needs. Therefore, they could go any length to acquire whatever thing they wanted. Pay attention to your thought whenever you begin to feel a pressing demand for something that is not yours. It could be an entitlement thinking error trying to creep into your thinking faculty. Learn to differentiate what you need from your wants. Do not allow greed to make you desire what is not supposed to be yours.

4. Power of Orientation

Power of orientation is the mindset that compares situations or other people from themselves as a difference between the strong and the weak. If a person with this criminal mind perceives you to be weak, he or she will do everything to hurt and exploit you. Nothing you do for a person with the power of orientation will ever look like help. People with the power of orientation thinking would try to dominate others and control their environment to shield their feeling of powerlessness.

They always want to be seen as the best in all things and situations. Therefore, they portray a picture of themselves as though they are doing well while others are nothing. These kinds of people rise up by bringing others down, making them feel less of themselves. Rather than focusing your attention on other people's weaknesses, focus on skills that make you more disciplined.

5. Super optimism

Super optimism is the belief in being invincible and getting away with anything. This criminal thinking error makes people fantasize that they will never be caught in a crime they are about to commit. Most people with this kind of mindset rely on past criminal events that they did without being caught. People with a criminal lifestyle for months or years often enjoy the feeling of their crime without considering the consequences later. They always convince themselves that there is always an escape route for them. However, super optimism fails and would not work at all times.

Nevertheless, one way to be free from this kind of thinking pattern is to explore the future implication of any criminal activity before the action. You must always be aware that any criminal act comes with consequences and sometimes these consequences could be very grievous.

6. Cognitive indolence

From the word 'indolence,' which means laziness, cognitive indolence entails lazy thinking. People with criminal minds are lazy in thought and this reflects in their actions. They always want shortcuts to achieve their hideous act and these often land them in trouble. Their mindset is oriented towards enjoying the short-term benefit of their crime rather than the long-term consequences of their criminal lifestyle. Criminal thinking of cognitive indolence enjoys the path of less resistance.

7. Discontinuity

One error in thinking is discontinuity. People with discontinuity thinking error are often distracted by their environment and lose sight of their goals easily. They could choose to change a habit but later fall victim to the same old habit because of something from their past that distracted them now. For instance, a criminal who manages to change his lifestyle could fall back into the same old pattern due to discontinuity thinking error.

CHAPTER SEVEN:
CHANGING YOUR BEHAVIOUR

"To change a habit, make a conscious decision, and then act out the new behavior."

- Maxwell Maltz

Can behavior be reset? Is it not part of our genetic makeup? Do you think resetting your behavior is almost impossible? Well, let me burst your bubbles. To cultivate a new behavior might not be easy, but that does not mean it is impossible. Do not say a thing is impossible unless you have tried it.

A behavioral change involves the coming together of various change steps that lead to the final act of doing something in a new way. The first step is to decide to act and then do it. Decision is the bedrock for every action. When action is repeated over time, it becomes a routine and then a habit. After many repetitions, you then say you have acquired a new behavior.

To effect change, you first have to acknowledge that your old behavior is not desirable. Then, your acknowledgment should be followed by an effort to correct the old habit. You want to change because there is a fault in your old habit. Possibly, something in your habit is limiting your progress or affecting your relationship with others. Now, to effect the change, you don't have to dwell on the bad behavior. Dwelling on what you do not like empowers it to keep taunting you. It creates a vicious cycle that leaves you to sink deeper into the mess it creates. You must realize that you are not bad. You have only just picked up a bad habit that can be corrected.

Therefore, you need to reset your behavior to its default state. Resetting your behavior is a significant end product of a changed way of thinking. After you have reset your mind and taught it to think differently, your actions and behaviors are supposed to reflect these changes. However, this is not always the case.

Old habits, they say, die hard, which is very true when it comes to moving from thoughts to actions. It is easier to change your thoughts than it is to change your behaviors. That is why the behavioral reset is another journey you need to embark on. In this journey, it is possible to see yourself taking a couple of steps backward after making some progress. You might find yourself jostling between acquiring a new behavior and sticking to your old ways. However, a strong desire for change should keep you on track. This is why behavioral change is not trying to fit your round peg into someone else's hole. If you try that, you would surely give up along the line.

The real behavioral change is becoming a better version of yourself and you must devote your life to it. With such devotion, the change you seek will eventually be achieved. It will take time and test your limits, but you can affect a change or behavioral reset if you really want it.

"We may think there is willpower involved, but more likely...
change is due to want power.
Wanting the new addiction more than the old one.
Wanting the new me in preference to the person I am now."

- George A. Sheehan

To reset your behavior through a change in your thinking pattern is always hard. But, you must be resilient to keep trying and consciously act in the new way of thinking. When you change the thoughts that feed your mind, you commit to doing things in a new way. For instance, you make goals and those goals make you when you stay disciplined with them. Another thing that begins to happen is that what entices you no longer appeal to you because something is already changing in your mind.

Nevertheless, due to the nature of your old habits being part of you for a long time, you may find that getting rid of them becomes a continuous struggle. For instance, a little trigger of a nude scene to a pornography addict could bring alive that old behavior. So, you must avoid every form of a person or things that could stand as a trigger for your old behavior if you truly want a changed life.

Consequently, it takes more than motivation to change an old habit. You must be disciplined about what you want and remain consistent with it. One thing you should bear in mind is that for any change to occur, every step on the way is significant. For instance, if you have decided to change behaviors that affect your health negatively, you must choose to rest more, exercise more, eat healthier and avoid smoking or drinking. These decisions represent a lifestyle change. The desire to change mostly emanates from the negative effects of engaging in the previous destructive lifestyle. You need to get to the end of yourself to desire a new you.

The story of the prodigal son is truly a perfect picture of how you can reset your behavior. The boy asked his father to give him the portion of the father's inheritance due to him. The purpose for this was to go lavish all he inherited. The boy had wasteful behavior and spent both his time and money on what did not profit him. It is so saddening that he spent all and was left with none. His behavior almost ruined him until he opted for change.

The Bible says,

> *"I will arise and go to my father, and will say to him, "Father, I have sinned against heaven and before you, and I am no longer worthy to be called your son. Make me like one of your hired servants."*

- Luke 15:18-19

Awesome! You change when you get to the end of yourself. The prodigal son's story is an important message to every young man and woman reading this right now. I know you have a zeal to explore. There is a burning desire in your heart to live as you like. But you need to take caution. Any act or behavior you engage in now could either make or mar you for life at this young age. Young people are full of mistakes; the old is full of regret. If you do not want to regret it later in your life, live in a very dignified way.

SETBACKS TO BEHAVIORAL CHANGES

"Wanting the new me in preference to the person I am right now."

- George Sheehan

One of the major setbacks of behavioral changes is to dwell on the negative side as the reason you want to change. Negative drives do not encourage long-lasting changes in behaviors. Changes that are driven by fear, shame, and regret do not persist. At any point in time when the feeling of shame, regret, or fear keeps staring you to the face, you will find yourself indulging in the old destructive habits you have once forgotten.

So, a successful change of behavioral pattern is based on positive thinking. This implies that your thoughts focus on the benefits of the new behavior rather than the old errors.

Consequently, to reset your behaviors, you have to be specific about what you're giving up and what you want to achieve. Vague descriptions of goals leave room for the incorporation of the old behavior. If you decide to quit a behavior, be specific about it. For example, saying, "I want to stop drinking alcohol to save my liver" or "I will go for a walk for 30 minutes every day to keep in shape" is a more specific goal than saying, "I'm going to cut down on drinking" or "I'm going to walk for a few minutes."

A loose interpretation of the words "cutting down on alcohol" would still make you indulge in the habit. You convince yourself that you are taking much less than you're used to, but the habit goes on. A few minutes of walking can be five minutes. Without specific goals, the body is bound to relapse into old habits. You must ensure that your behavioral changes goals are specific and watertight, leaving no room for false interpretations.

Too many behavioral changes at the same time can also be a challenge. It becomes hard to keep up with them all at once. Your willpower has a limit and when you push it beyond its limit, it will so happen that you will find comfort in an old destructive habit. Too many changes at the same time is not productive. Establish practical ways to discard old habits and cultivating new ones. You aim to quit alcohol? Do away with the alcoholic drinks you have in your possession. Designate an activity or a substitute for every time you feel the need to satisfy the urge.

A lot of research has gone into understanding changes in behavior and how you can effectively change behaviors. This has led to theories about how change occurs, the components of change, and the stages involved in changes. These theories do not explain all there is to behavioral changes. Still, it provides a useful roadmap to understanding what you're dealing with.

There are three elements of change you need to consider in resetting your behavior. The first is your readiness to change. If you are not ready and willing to change, there is little that can be done. Readiness implies putting the resources that will make a reset in behavior lasting. Willingness is the desire to change. You must acquire both the resources and the willingness to change.

The second element is the barriers to change. Some obstacles have been erected in your life over time that will make changing old behaviors difficult. They could be mental and emotional desires that trigger a repeat of that behavior. Identify such barriers and delete them. This leads to the third and final element of change, the likelihood of a relapse. If the second element is not removed, it leads to the third element. They are what trigger a repeat of old behaviors. These three elements of change are important if you want to successfully reset your behavior.

THE STAGES OF CHANGE

The Transtheoretical Model, regarded as one of the best approaches to studying change, was introduced in the 1970s by James Prochaska and Carlo DiClemente to help people quit smoking. Their research developed this model, which has since been useful in understanding how people go through behavioral changes.

According to the model, change occurs gradually, and setbacks and relapses are regarded as part of the process. It also postulates that people are unwilling and resists changes in the early stages instead of the later stages when they develop a proactive approach. The stages of change include the following;

1. Precontemplation

The characteristics of people in this stage are denial, ignorance of the problem and a lack of information. This is the earliest stage of behavioral reset. At this stage, you have no conscious intention of making any change, either due to ignorance, a lack of information, or plain denial of the existence of bad behavior.

The apparent lack of intention could also stem from the previous failure. In this stage, you avoid reading, discussing, or talking about the behavior. However, you are aware of it by external interests, influence from others, public information, or others' stories that highlight the problem you're facing. It is common to deny the harmful effects of this behavior. Unless informed, you will continue going down this path.

To exit this stage, you must ask yourself questions. Have you at any time tried to change this behavior? Do you consider this behavior problematic? What consequences can stem from this behavior that will make you consider it a problem? Honest answers to this will help you move past precontemplation a change. Get a sense of what this behavior is preventing you from achieving.

2. Contemplation

At this stage, you are more aware of the benefits of a behavior change. There is a struggle between balancing the potential benefits and the cost of making the change. This rising conflict brings about ambivalence that is a characteristic of this stage. This conflict tends to last for a long time because you view the cost as giving up something rather than gaining something.

The contemplation stage is usually the place where most changes die naturally. You must move past this phase if you're intent on making the change. Do not dwell on the negatives of the change but rather consider the positives of that change. Weigh the pros and cons carefully. Ask the right questions and you will get the right answers that will help you leave the contemplation stage.

3. Preparation

You are now aware that you must change and you believe that you can. You make preparations for this change and make little efforts that show your desire for change. Obstacles to your change become visible at this point and you must identify and avoid such obstacles.

In this stage, you must take certain steps to ensure you remain on track. Collect necessary information about changing your behavior, writing down goals, and a list of motivating reasons. Encouragements and advice from friends, support groups, church leaders can also go a long way.

4. Action

The action stage is where you take direct action towards changing. You've stopped engaging in the old habits and you are engaged in new productive and healthy habits. There is the danger of relapse in this stage if the previous stages are not properly dealt with. You are faced with the challenges of abandoning old habits and might be tempted to fall back. Create rewards for yourself, engage in positive thinking and talks to yourself. Once again, seek support.

5. Maintenance

In this stage, you have successfully avoided former behaviors and habits. You, therefore, aim to keep it this way. Avoid tempting situations. Replace old behaviors with new positive ones, lest you fall back into the old ways. Engage more in reward for action every time you avoid a relapse. In case you fail, be reminded that change is a process and you are well on your way to it. Do not demoralize yourself; that will only sink you deeper.

Over time, progression through the stages of change is not linear and relapse is common. This is called the Spiral Model of the Changes. Although it is rare to move back to the first stage, relapses serve as a learning curve and help plan for the next stage.

RESETTING YOUR BEHAVIORS AS A BELIEVER

The first thing you must realize is that God loves you as his child. God's help is readily available for you whenever you need it. This is your advantage in the struggle for a reset. The knowledge that you have God on your side is encouraging and gives you the zeal to fight for the changes. All you need to do is to look into the truth of God's word, establish them in your life and apply them.

As a believer, you must realize that you are dead to your old nature and had taken upon yourself a new life. Apostle Paul puts it this way;

"I have been crucified with Christ; it is no longer I who live, but Christ lives in me; and the life which I now live in the flesh I live by faith in the Son of God, who loved me and gave Himself for me."

- Galatians 2:20

At salvation, you have a new life, different from the way you used to live. What marks the difference is that God's spirit now directs you on the choices, decisions, and manner you need to live. Your old nature of sin is death. This is the consequence of receiving Christ. When you accepted Jesus Christ as your Lord and savior, you gave up all your bad behavior. There was an exchange of your old way of life for a new one.

You must reckon yourself dead to the old nature. There ought to be a sense of belief in your spirit that this is true. Only then can you start manifesting the life that you desire. Motivation is not enough. Some strategies are laid out to deal with behavior changes and they work. Still, as Christians, these strategies may not account for the behavioral changes you desire. That is why you need to tap into the power of your faith to make such changes.

The scripture is very clear on dealing with old habits and desires.

"But put on the Lord Jesus Christ, and make no provision for the flesh, to fulfill its lusts."

- Romans 13:14

Biblical principles are not out of touch with men's principles because even the Bible was written by men as they were moved by the Holy Ghost. Often, principles that work in our world were biblical principles modified to fit into the world system. You see that both principles advised that you make no provision for triggers of old habits or behaviors. The Bible was specific enough to tell us how avoidance can be a means of behavioral reset.

To reset your behavior, surrender your human nature to God and He will lead you through every day by the power of the Holy Spirit. The Holy Spirit will initiate the lifestyle changes you desire holistically. Reckon that you have left the old nature behind by virtue of your acceptance into the body of Christ.

Always begin with prayer. Prayer breaks every yoke, including that of destructive behavior. When you are fed up with that behavior and desire to change, prayer is the best place to begin to demand that change. Admit that your flesh is weak and can only be made strong through the power of God. Come to God in prayer and he will help you overcome. Believe that you are rid of this sin by believing Jesus.

You should note that the principles and theories outlined work in tandem with the Bible's principles. Still, without the biblical principles, you will be running in circles. A reset is only complete through the help of the Holy Spirit and the word of God that is made manifest in your life.

CHAPTER EIGHT:
BLEEDING OUT

To help you understand the concept of bleeding, a more physical and realistic representation will be used to describe it. There's so much insight to gain from the doctor's perspective and it will be used to explain the phenomenon 0f bleeding out in your life as a believer.

THE MEDICAL VIEW

The first thing to note here is that bleeding can be fatal. Bleeding has been known to claim the lives of so many victims. So, it is something not to be trifled with. In the United States, a review showed that each year, 60,000 Americans die from blood loss. On the world scale, the number rises to 2 million. Bleeding out from wounds and injuries is not something you want.

Now, before we get lost in the medical world, I want you to relate some problems, habits, or situations around your life to mean injuries. These situations or ways of life and thinking have been known to cause discomfort and loss in various aspects of your life. So, if these situations persist over time, then you are likely to be bleeding as a result. The risks are even greater for believers because you have chosen to live an exceptional kind of life, but managing this bleeding with your new life could be so problematic and tiring. This can be so fatal that it seems you are losing your life.

Bleeding can be so fatal when a vital organ is involved. It could lead to death within a matter of minutes if not carefully arrested. The veins and some critical internal organs are terrible places to sustain injuries. You do not want to sustain injuries in such areas as the liver or heart. If injuries in these organs are left unattended for too long, the victim could bleed to death in minutes.

Also, there are situations of internal bleeding where an organ is ruptured internally without any external wound. This is a very fatal form of bleeding since the victim cannot even tell if there is a problem. The thing with bleeding out is that the process itself is not very painful and can go unnoticed. The injuries are where the pain ends. Beyond that, bleeding out can seem to be a very regular occurrence, causing serious harm.

Likewise, sin is likened to the case of injuries that causes bleeding. For a Christian, the process of cultivating a bad habit or living in a way that is contrary to God's precepts can seem harmless and pleasurable, but the end result is death. If you're a devout believer, you will feel a sense of pain and disturbance when you start thinking and acting in a way that's contrary to the way of God. But after a while, that pain fades off if you allow it to take over you.

You see, our conscience is the first regulator of our thoughts and actions. However, if you give yourself to an action that causes you to sin, you gradually quiet your conscience and silence your spirit.

A believer who still falls victim to addiction is bleeding. Such a person needs healing.

The Bible says;

> *"For when we were in the flesh, the sinful passions which were aroused by the law were at work in our members to bear fruit to death."*

- Romans 7:5

Being saved means you have chosen a new life and had embraced the gift of Jesus to humanity. It implies that you have resolved to forgo your old ways of living in sin and obey God's word to the letter. But along the line, the desires of your flesh still draw you into acts that do not glorify God or reflect the new life in Christ. Although you are saved, you are still bleeding because of habits formed in your heart due to years of accumulated thoughts and actions that fuel the habit.

These habits do not just affect any random aspect of your life. They affect t the crucial and most important ones, which we can also refer to as the vital organs of your life. Your spirit, mind, and health are vital parts of you that become damaged due to constant exposure to demeaning thoughts and habits.

You can suffer from internal bleeding when you do not realize that your habits are causing harm to important aspects of your life. If it happens and you are not aware of the dangers of a situation you have placed yourself, then bleeding out is imminent.

NEGATIVE THINKING AND HABITS

Negative thinking is like a trap that ensnares its victim. Like a trap, it sinks its teeth deeper into the victim with time, causing blood loss and subsequently a slow death. There are two types of victims in this trap. These are;

- ✓ The comfortable Victim
- ✓ The Silent Victim

The comfortable victim is the one who feels relaxed in the trap of negative thoughts or habits because they are pleasurable. He or she sees the detriments of being in that situation but still derives pleasure that makes him or her reluctant to call for help. Such people would refuse to acknowledge that their thinking and way of life are the reason for the major setbacks.

The other type of victim is the Silent victim. The silent victim will be in pain and know it but will refuse to cry out for help. As a result, this person suffers the consequences of being trapped.

Just as trapped animals more often die from a loss of blood, so is it with these victims who are entrapped in behaviors or situation that causes harm. Many people are bleeding out because of their situations and manner of thinking. Still, they have refused to arrest this situation. Suppose you are in this position of struggling with a way of life, a bad habit, or an addiction. In that case, you can choose to do something about your situation today to not suffer loss.

The loss in these situations could be financial loss, spiritual loss, or even mental loss. The good news is that you can be free from unhealthy habits and lifestyles that slowly drain your resources and energy. God's intent for you is a balance and wholesome life. You were made to live life and live it fully.

However, the devil would not want that for you. Little wonder the scriptures say;

"The thief (the devil) does not come except to steal, and to kill, and to destroy. I have come that they may have life and that they may have it more abundantly."

- John 10:10

The abundant life is God's plan for every believer. Therefore, if you are in a situation or you are struggling with a way of life that does not accomplish these, you're in a trap and must cry out to avoid bleeding out to death. These struggles are but machinations of the thief (the devil) so that he can destroy your life. When you remain silent, you give the devil an advantage over the situation.

Jesus paid for your sins, struggles and difficulties on the cross. He didn't shed his blood on that cross, only for you to bleed out again. Therefore, you must call on the power of his sacrifice to put an end to every struggle in your life and set you free indeed. You are uniquely positioned as God's child to handle anything the devil throws at you because you have Jesus. Jesus' presence in your life is what you need to break free totally.

"And suddenly, a woman who had a flow of blood for twelve years came from behind and touched the hem of His garment. For she said to herself, "If only I may touch His garment, I shall be made well."

- **Matthew 9:20-21**

The woman with the issue of blood knew the power in accessing God's provision for her healing through Jesus Christ. Some people refer to this woman as the bleeding woman. Of course, she suffered from continuous bleeding for 12 years. In her time, a bleeding woman was regarded as unclean. She had to stay away from the synagogue and other people. She was practically declared a "persona non grata" amongst her own people.

Imagine living and being isolated for most of your life. But this woman had faith. Instead of bleeding out for the rest of her life, the bleeding woman sought help in the right place and she was cured of her ailment forever.

Sometimes, you should learn to acknowledge your problem if you truly want a solution for it. Without acknowledgment, there can be no freedom from a bad way of life. Recognizing the harm done by a certain way of life you have been living or certain situations you find yourself in is the most important step you must take in the struggle to change things. Without it, the damage being done continues. Acknowledging the harm and then seeking help are keys to changing any negative situation or way of thinking you have discovered.

"He who covers his sins will not prosper, but whoever confesses and forsakes them will have mercy."

- Proverbs 28:13

When you refuse to acknowledge your shortcomings but prefer to hide them and claim ignorance, you will keep wallowing in its hurt. It is easier to put away your issues than to deal with them. If you don't deal with them, they will continue to grow and cause damage and sometimes, these damages are irreparable. You must take a conscious decision to acknowledge these shortcomings and deal with them accordingly.

"Therefore, do not let sin reign in your mortal body, that you should obey it in its lusts. And do not present your members as [d]instruments of unrighteousness to sin, but present yourselves to God as being alive from the dead, and your members as instruments of righteousness to God. For sin shall not have dominion over you, for you are not under law but under grace."

- Romans 6:12 - 14

When you choose to remain in a detrimental situation without seeking change, you are more likely to bleed out and consequently suffer loss. As we have seen, this is not God's plan for you. Many people bleed out due to a refusal to leave or change a habit or way of life that is not helpful to their lives. It is common to see negatives propped up, packaged and accepted as normal.

As a Christian, you should discern and distinguish what helps you grow from what harms your spiritual life. You should endeavor to leave a place of struggle and old habits behind lest they drag you down, cut you deeper and bleed you out.

SEEK HELP FOR YOUR SITUATION

"Now, a certain woman had a flow of blood for twelve years, 26 and had suffered many things from many physicians. She had spent all that she had and was no better but rather grew worse."

- Mark 5:25-26

The bleeding woman had one thing on her mind when she discovered that Jesus was passing by on that fateful day she got her healing. She wanted her healing. She needed help. We are also meant to see that she did not keep quiet about her problem from the passage. She had sought help from several doctors and caregivers in a bid to find a lasting solution.

The woman with the issue of blood acknowledged her problem and drew the attention of those who could solve it. She had a desire to change and was resolute until she saw the change. Her story teaches a very important lesson to every believer. You would think that after 12 years of suffering from that ailment, she would resign to fate. But no, this woman was persistent for a change, even when the situation was getting worse. It was in her bid to find a solution that she came in contact with Jesus. My dear reader, I urge you to never lose hope in yourself. Seek what you want until you find it.

When you acknowledge a problem in your life, you must do all it takes to find a solution. It matters little how long this change will take, but the desire to see that it happens is one that you must cultivate. You must find a lasting solution to any problem confronting you right now and not just some quick means of escape.

Subsequently, when it looks as if you are losing out in the struggle for a change, do not be tempted to cover up your failure from those who can actually help you. Do not hide your shortcomings because only then will you be able to find a solution. God works in mysterious ways, and you can find healing through anyone he chooses. Hiding your transgression is tantamount to ignoring them on purpose and wishing they would go away.

The bleeding woman sought help from Jesus and was healed. She had sought help from various places (a commendable act, none of which worked) until she met Jesus. There is only one stop for your bleedings as a child of God. You need not search too far or too wide, bearing in mind that he is more than capable of changing our ways and situation. He lived as we did and conquered sin.

"Seeing then that we have a great High Priest who has passed through the heavens, Jesus the Son of God, let us hold fast our confession. For we do not have a High Priest who cannot sympathize with our weaknesses, but was in all points tempted as we are, yet without sin. Let us therefore come boldly to the throne of grace, that we may obtain mercy and find grace to help in time of need."

- Hebrews 4:14-16

Your help will only come from God. Seek his help, seek him out and you will find a lasting solution to your bleedings. Jesus Christ has bled for every believer on the cross and as such, you should not be bleeding out from a shortcoming. His footsteps and life here on earth are a guide to the type of life you want to emulate. Seek him out like the bleeding woman did and he shall make the changes required to stop your bleeding.

CHAPTER NINE:
THE 8 ATTITUDES OF CHANGE

"Attitude is a little thing that makes a big difference."

- Winston Churchill

Attitude is everything. A problem becomes insurmountable or not due to your attitude towards it. With the right attitude, you will get your desired results. So, attitude is everything. It determines the height you get to in life. Your skill can get you to the top, but attitude helps you retain the top position. The truth is, what you call a problem is not actually the problem. The real deal is your attitude about the problem. What is your perception of it? Do you see a problem as a means to serve humanity or as an impossible feat?

Subsequently, doggedness, zeal and a will to carry on are some of the attitudes exhibited by those who have achieved great things. And in so many different situations, cultivating the right attitude will not only help you learn some new and improved characters. It will also help you achieve the necessary results. You just have to figure out the attitude you need to achieve your results.

Attitude is the key to unlocking your desires. It is not enough to want a thing; you must be willing and pay the price for it. Everything worthwhile comes with a price and the price is affordable when you have the right attitude towards it. The attitude of persistence opens any door. Keep being positive about what you want until it becomes a reality in your life.

Sometimes, the challenge is that what you want might take time and challenges around it might make you feel it is not for you. However, the right attitude is to keep at it until you see the result you desire. Resilience is an attitude of winners. If you quit when you ought to persist, you have failed.

Your attitude reveals your stance towards overcoming that obstacle. Your attitude reveals what you're made of. It shows how you face challenging situations and how you intend to rise from your lurch. With the wrong attitude, no matter the resources and strategies you throw at a problem, it remains the same. The right attitude makes your little idea the brightest.

"Nothing can stop the man with the right mental attitude from achieving his goal; nothing on earth can help the man with the wrong mental attitude."

- Thomas Jefferson

With the right attitude, your only limit is yourself. Everything else is subject to the attitude you carry. That is why you must hone the ideal attitude to combat every challenging situation uniquely. Identify the problems and the attitude needed to overcome them.

Having the right attitudes will reveal whether or not you are capable of changing your thinking in the long term or not. There are strategies for changing your thinking, but only with the right attitude will you learn and perfect them.

Your attitude influences your actions. It differentiates a successful person from a failure. Do you know that attitude determines who truly wins in the race of life? The difference between the happy and fulfilled deliveryman next door and the top manager next street who feels frustrated about everything is attitude. While the former finds fulfillment in what he does, the latter found stress and pain in his. There is nothing wrong with being a top manager, CEO, and business owner. What you must know is the perspective from where you see your job? Do you see it as a job or a fulfillment of purpose? Do you see your profession as another opportunity to serve humanity or a 9-5 compulsory duty? This is why attitude is everything.

To change your attitude, you need to cultivate these eight (8) attitudes of change. These attitudes are what you need to successfully incorporate a new way of thinking into your life. If you lack these attitudes, a change in thinking will be difficult to obtain. They are basic foundations upon which a reset of the mind, actions and behaviors are built open. You must understand these attitudes and seek them in your everyday endeavors to activate a change in your thinking manner.

ATTITUDE OF GRATITUDE

"Gratitude turns what we have into enough and more. It turns denial into acceptance, chaos into order, confusion into clarity...it makes sense of our past, brings peace for today, and creates a vision for tomorrow."

- Melody Beattie

A heart of gratitude is thankful for everything. A grateful heart appreciates even the slightest gesture done. Gratitude is an important attitude to develop because it changes how you see things and how you think about people and things. With an attitude of gratitude, you will always see things in a good light. Gratitude makes you see possibility and positivity. You don't see the difficulties in situations; instead, you see the blessings, opportunities and things to be thankful for.

Gratitude shifts the focus from always thinking about yourself and your problems to thinking about something else or someone else's problem so that you can find a way to bring them out of it. A grateful heart sees God in all situations and every living soul. If you are grateful, you will not talk down or backlash anyone because everything you see and have will look to you as a privilege from God.

An attitude of gratitude gravitates you towards positivity and less negativity. Your mindset and thinking are always tuned in to positivity regardless of the situation or the things happening around you. With an attitude of gratitude, your thinking does not recognize the difficulties; it only recognizes blessings and reasons to be grateful. When you cultivate the attitude of gratitude, you feel positive, feel at peace, and are not bogged down by the earth's complaints and troubles, not because they aren't there, but your thinking has been shifted. You are always aware of the great things going on in your life.

> *"Be thankful for what you have; you'll end up having more. If you concentrate on what you don't have, you will never, ever have enough."*
>
> **- Oprah Winfrey**

Gratitude makes you compassionate, you feel happier, you focus on the things and people that matter in your life. It is such an important attitude to cultivate. When most people are bothered about the way things are and beseeched by negative thoughts that do nothing to help them, you are full of positivity because you have found a way to develop positive thinking. Your way of thinking has changed.

Gratitude improves your self-esteem and self-confidence. You begin to find pleasure in the little things and the good moments you have. Gratitude means you focus less on worrying about what you lack and more on what you have available.

THE BURDEN OF RESPONSIBILITY

"If you can take responsibility for your own life, then you will begin to realize that you can change it."

- H. K. Abell

Responsibility is a character or attitude that is essential to the growth of every individual. It is critical to the way you think and approaches things. Responsibility affects how you handle situations and respond to challenges and difficulties. Responsibility means being accountable for action. It is an obligation to take action, control a situation or do something to your own benefit.

Developing an attitude of responsibility means you do not put the blame of a situation on others. Instead, you are focused on doing something to change that situation. Your thinking changes from that of a blame pattern of thinking to a solution-oriented way of thinking. You think about a way out, not the cause of the problem. Developing a sense of responsibility is critical to changing your way of thinking.

Suppose you do not develop this attitude of responsibility. In that case, your life affairs are left to chance and you tend to blame others for your irresponsibility. The blame culture is a terrible way of thinking that will not change if you don't take responsibility. Your life, in general, will not change if you don't take responsibility.

Today, the world is rooted in blame; if you want to make changes, you must take responsibility. If you want to achieve a change in the way you think, cultivate a responsible attitude. The attitude of responsibility is a commitment to change the way you live, think and the outcome of your life. No one who desires change in any aspect of life remains irresponsible. It is a step towards tangible action that results in a changed way of thinking, mindset and behavior. Do you desire to change? Be responsible for it

CARING HEART

"Never believe that a few caring people can't change the world. For, indeed, that's all who ever have."

-Margaret Mead

Caring is the attitude of concern and interest. Without a caring attitude, you will not be interested in any form of change. Care is a very significant attitude. When it is lacking, there is no desire to effect change. If you don't care, you won't see a need to change your way of thinking or how things are happening in your life.

Caring is closely related to irresponsibility. When you care about something, you show interest in it, and you learn about it. If you want to change, you must show concern. You must desire it to learn.

Whatever you care for is important to you and it is a criterion through which God speaks to his people. Everyone who has ever made great leaps cared about something. Desires become a reality when the heart cares for something important to it.

WILLINGNESS

"If you are willing and obedient, you shall eat the good of the land."

- Isaiah 1:19

This is one of the most critical attitudes that drive change. The attitude of willingness speaks about desire. God wants these two from us⊠willingness and obedience. He knows that a willing heart will be receptive to obey. You cannot be willing if you do not have an intention to have. What do you desire to have? How much of it do you want? When do you want it? The answer to all these questions is your extent of willingness.

If you are willing, no price will be too great to pay for greatness or to have what you want. Willingness is the hunger in your heart to achieve the desired goal. A willing heart is ready to get involved and do what is necessary to achieve a change of mind or situation.

Willingness is desire, even in the face of mounting challenges. The end product or the desire for the out product far outweighs whatever challenge lies in front. Adopting a willing attitude prepares you to take on the challenges of change. Without a willing attitude, you will falter under the slightest pressure. Willingness makes you persist because you desire that change. You want a change in that situation. Willingness depends on your motivation to learn and to change.

> *"The willingness to experiment with change may be the most essential ingredient to success at anything."*

> **- Pat Summit**

When you're willing to act, things work in favor of your decision. Unwillingness shows a resignation to accept whatever situation or position you find yourself. Willingness shows the hunger and needs to improve a way of life, thinking, or the outcome of a situation. Willingness is an essential attitude for change. With it comes an increase in the desire to do more and achieve more.

OPEN MINDEDNESS

This is an attitude that many claim to have, but it is found to be lacking when tested. This is the major stumbling block of change, if any kind, a refusal to be open-minded. When a need for change arises, an open-minded attitude is what keeps you from doing what you've been doing all along. It is an attitude that allows the acceptance of new ways of thinking.

Open-mindedness is the willingness to search, discover and accept the evidence for change of one's way of thinking, beliefs of a way of life. It is an ability to accept change from different sources and people. It doesn't by any stretch mean being easily swayed by new information or new ideas. It is a careful process of checking through a new process fairly without bias and accepting such an idea's merits.

It is an attitude that encourages growth immensely. Open-mindedness does not signify indecisiveness, neither does it signify a lack of ability to think independently. Rather it indicates the ability to weigh reasonable alternatives and make a suitable choice.

An open-minded person is receptive to new ideas and ways of doing things that do not favor their initial beliefs. It goes without saying that such an attitude is critical to making a change. The reverse of open-mindedness is being biased towards already existing beliefs.

HONESTY

"Every lie is two lies, the lie we tell others and the lie we tell ourselves to justify it."

--Robert Brault

Honesty is the ability to see the truth, accept it, and speaks the truth to yourself and others. Only through honesty can you admit there is a need for change. When you make a careful assessment of your situation and face the real decisive questions, only an honest assessment or attitude will provide you with the answers you need.

Dishonesty to yourself hinders you from change. Dishonesty towards others prevents you from learning and developing. To initiate the change, you need to learn and without honesty, learning becomes tasking. And you know that without learning, then there is no platform to initiate change.

"True honesty is hard. Throughout my career, I've faced moments where I've needed to take an honest look at myself and face some very uncomfortable realities."

- Les Brown

The truth is, honesty will let you make some choices that are hard but rewarding in the end. But the hardest point is the point of change. Do not lower your standard of honesty just to blend in. Nothing changes when you blend. It is only a disguise. Keep being honest and you will experience a transformation in your mentality that will reflect in your life.

HUMILITY

Humility is the character of evaluating yourself modestly. It signifies a low or moderate view of your abilities, instead insisting that you are eager to learn and improve your existing abilities.

The opposite of humility is pride. To learn, you must be humble. Pride does not favor learning. It is an obstruction to change and improvement. A proud individual believes he or she knows all there is to know and knows better than anyone else. It is difficult for a proud person to be open to change. Arrogance and unwillingness to learn are products of pride. Change is difficult with pride, but with humility, willingness comes easy and change is easily obtainable.

"Humility is the true key to success. Successful people lose their way at times. They often embrace and overindulge from the fruits of success. Humility halts this arrogance and self-indulging trap. Humble people share the credit and wealth, remaining focused and hungry to continue the journey of success."

- Rick Pittino

A prime example of a humble man is Jesus. Despite his capabilities and status, he was welcoming, humble and lived amongst sinners and believers alike. He came down from heaven, let His throne and all, just to die for mankind because of his humility. Humility prepares you to serve and in service, there is reward. Jesus is God, but that did not stop him from being a servant to the people. He serves humanity to the point of losing his life in that servitude. Jesus set the perfect example of what humility is about (1 peter 5:5-7).

OBJECTIVITY

"Your life must focus on the maximization of objectivity."

- Charlie Munger

To initiate change in your life or way of thinking, you need to learn to look at situations objectively without any sense of bias. You will be unable to do things differently or approach difficult situations without being objective. Objectivity is an attitude that encourages change. In its absence, bias thrives and this prevents you from making correct analysis and decisions.

The lack of objectivity is like having a roadblock to your thinking. It muddies your thoughts. This is an attitude that makes you consider every new idea fairly. You make judgments without the inclination to favor a specific outcome because you are not stuck on one idea. Any path chosen must be backed with considerable information to indicate it is the right one. A lack of objectivity signals a certain attachment to a way of life that prevents people from taking a different change approach.

Now that you had seen the eight attitudes needed for change. I would like you to identify anyone lagging in your life and make amends as soon as possible. Change is not a one-time event. As you grow, you learn and change. Let these attitudes become a core value of your life as you advance in life.

CHAPTER TEN :
SATAN'S AGENDA

Let me start by telling you that Satan is real and his operation is evident among mankind. In the past and now, many theologies undermine Satan's manifestation (sometimes called the devil) in humanity's affair. They tend to say that ever since the devil was cast out of heaven, he has no power over men's affairs. But this theology is not true.

The devil moved around to and fro the earth (Job 2:2). He tempted Jesus during Jesus' earthly ministry on earth (Luke 4:1-13). The devil is the cause for all evil practices on earth. He has a mission to steal, kill and destroy (John 10:10) and his target is mankind who were made in God's image. So, you should not ignore the fact that there is a devil that is constantly against your life so that he could bring you down in all ways.

Now, the balance here is that the devil is real. But what is more real is our victory through Christ Jesus. The Bible says;

"For whatever is born of God overcomes the world. And this is the victory that has overcome the world — our faith. Who is he who overcomes the world, but he who believes that Jesus is the Son of God?"

- 1 John 5:4-5

The devil had been in constant warfare against God and His works. You can trace this to the devil's appeal that made Adam and Eve sin against God in the Garden of Eden. Until now, the devil had not ceased warring against mankind just to make us sin against God and fall short of God's glory. But the good news is that God had given us victory over the devil through faith in the person of Jesus.

Your victory is sealed by faith in Christ Jesus. This implies that your life is no longer by the devil's dictates but by what God's word says and promised you. I smile when I see the devil trying to attack my mind against God's will. The same strategy the devil had been using since the inception of the world is today. The Devil uses the lust of the flesh, the lust of the eyes and the pride of life as his strategy for an attack against humanity. Once you can understand the devil's operational style, you have gained victory over him.

Consequently, I will like us to further study who Satan, the devil is if you truly want to understand his agenda. The devil is a liar (John 8:44). He will present to you God's word in a very deceptive way, just the same way he did for Eve when he told her, "You will not surely die." (Genesis 3:5). Not only does the devil lie and deceive, but he also kills and destroys. He will whisper to your mind thoughts that would make you see yourself above God Almighty and allow pride to take over your life.

Dear reader, do not give the devil a space in your thought, or else he would take over your whole life and draw you away from God and His word. The devil is always anti-God and he would do anything possible just to distract you from God. Today, there are lots of distractions in the form of lust but with advanced technology.

Now, I would not say that the advent of the internet is a bad thing because internet use had made people far and wide hear the gospel. If you are reading this book as an eBook, it is one of the many benefits of the internet.

However, the devil had hijacked this same great gift to humanity using the same old trick of lust to bring corruption to mind. This is why you see a lot of raunchy movies, pornography and luscious musical on the internet. The aim is to make you esteem pleasure over purpose, goodies over God and the works of the devil over the works of grace.

The truth is, the devil knows he cannot take you away from the church as a Christian. He knows he cannot keep you from studying your Bible. Satan knows he can't stop you from living the pious and sanctimonious Christian lifestyle. But you must not be ignorant of what the devil is capable of doing. The devil can make you get busy with so many activities that would keep you from consistent fellowship with Jesus. So, what the devil targets is not your life but your time.

Satan knows that if he can gain control over your time, he will control your life. The devil can keep you busy with non-essential things that you will eventually forget what you ought to be doing with your time. Time is what makes life worth living. Whatever stills your time with God has control over your life. The devil knows how to over-stimulate the human mind with all forms of enticing music, movies and television shows, so that you will no longer have time for prayers, meditation, or to develop intimacy with God.

On the other side, if you are too legalistic or overly spiritual with activities, you will indirectly be fueling your pride to receive men's praises, thinking it's God's will. You need to understand the motive behind your actions or else, you will be busy and guilty of the devil's vices.

How Satan Promotes His Agenda

"Whose minds the god of this age has blinded, who do not believe, lest the light of the gospel of the glory of Christ, who is the image of God, should shine on them."

- 2 Corinthians 4:4

God's word made it known that Satan is the 'god' of this world. It is evident by the way mankind gives priority to mundane pleasure and less attention to godliness. The love of God has waxed cold in the heart of many. But you wonder how Satan could captivate so many people who once pledged allegiance to God but are now subject to lust and carnality. The simple truth is the blindness of the mind, as seen in the above bible text.

The mind is the intermediary realm by which you can relate with the earth and the spirit realms. Whatever attacks that would come into a person's life are first targeted at the person's mind. Once the mind stops believing in certain truths of God's word, nothing anyone can do that would make the person get back to their right state of mind, except there is a certain work of grace. Satan promotes his agenda by different attacks on our minds.

Satan controls most of the thoughts and impulses that appeal so much to our sensuality, to take us far away from God. These thoughts become a life of sin the more we allow it to settle into our subconscious mind. Satan has several ways of getting these dangerous thoughts into man's heart so that he can expand his agenda among mankind. He does this in several ways. Below are some of these ways and how you can avoid them;

Ignorance

The Bible says;

"Having the understanding darkened, being alienated from the life of God through the ignorance that is in them, because of the blindness of their heart."

- Ephesian 4:18

The devil promotes his agenda through ignorance. Ignorance is a powerful tool the devil uses to ensure believers do not come to the knowledge of the truth of God's word. What you do not know, you cannot defend. The devil does hide the truth from us and make it look like some of the promises God had made for mankind are not true and the condition for fulfilling them is unrealistic. Out of ignorance, we accept the devil's lie and keep living under his dictates for long.

Subsequently, the devil has his agents called demons, who are master craft in manipulation. The devil knows that we would quest to seek knowledge. SO, he introduced false teaching among believers by manipulating the mind of the supposed teachers of God's word.

The truth is that ignorance is not only the lack of knowledge but also the expression of falsehood. The devil brings up false teachers who would teach, just to consume it upon their lust and selfish desires (James 4:3, 2 Peter 2:1-3). Now, you need to understand that Jesus is the only way to God-not anyone else or anything else.

Also, you must give yourself to personal study of God's word and prayers, especially in the Holy Ghost. These will keep you from the agenda of ignorance the devil has for mankind. Nevertheless, you will need to sustain your understanding of God's word through consistency.

Deception

A deception is a major tool the devil uses to promote his agenda on earth. It was the same deception he used at the beginning that is still applicable now. The devil is a master at deception that he would make you begin to doubt the truth you once have received if you are not careful. To be deceived is to believe a lie. Deception keeps you from knowing, let alone walking in the will of God for our life.

The recent deception of the devil is to believe in legalism rather than the gospel of Christ. Legalism depends on moral laws than faith in Christ. Hence, the focus will no longer be Christ. You must be careful not to allow the devil to make you think that it is acceptable to God once it is a good thing to do. Many good acts are not right before God. Therefore, keep learning at the feet of Jesus until you rise to that stature of Christ.

How not to be deceived by the Devil

"Beloved, do not believe every spirit, but test the spirits, whether they are of God; because many false prophets have gone out into the world."

- 1 John 4:1

Below are some of the ways to avoid being deceived by the devil;

-Stay with Sound Doctrine and teaching of God's word. The simplicity of God's word is essential for sound doctrine. Be careful about any teaching that sounds too mystical or weird.

- ✓ Be willing to give up your doctrine for Bible doctrine.
- ✓ Avoid pride. Know what you need to still know and learn in humility.
- ✓ Examine everything you believe in light of God's word.
- ✓ Trust the Holy Spirit inside of you to lead you on.
- ✓ Seek the kingdom of God through prayer, fasting and giving
- ✓ Don't hold on to traditions - it makes the word ineffective

- ✓ Receive the Word of God no matter what
- ✓ Put the Word first place
- ✓ Hide the Word in your heart and keep it on your lips and meditate in your mind.

The Control of Media

"In which you once walked according to the course of this world, according to the prince of the power of the air, the spirit who now works in the sons of disobedience."

- Ephesians 2:2

Indeed, Satan is in control of the airwaves (radio and television broadcast). How do I know this? Several radio and television broadcasts promote everything that is anti-God, anti-Christ, and against God's word. Gradually, programs like this infiltrate our minds and subtly corrupt them.

The devil knows that the gateway into the mind is through the things we hear and watch. Therefore, he would circulate into different media platforms dangerous content to corrupt the mind. The best time to guide your mind against the corruption of the devil is now.

Interestingly, the advent of social media had now made it worse that you do not have to walk into a gas station to pick up sex videos. The devil had made it available with just a click from your phone.

"Then He said to them, "Take heed what you hear. With the same measure you use, it will be measured to you; and to you who hear, more will be given."

- Mark 4:24

You can control what you watch and not allow the corruption of the devil to seep into your mind. Attach value to what you hear and see. Feed on words and videos that would help you love God more and grow into deep intimacy with Him. Be intentional about studying God's word and listening to message videos and clips that drive you to your knees in prayers.

Remember, Satan's agenda might vary from generation to generation. Still, his strategies are the same—the lust of the eyes, the lust of the flesh and the pride of life. Submit yourself to God and you will not gratify the lust of your flesh. Lust is subtle but destructive. It seeps into your mind like a frog in boiling water, which keeps adjusting itself to accommodate the heat until it can no longer do that. Keep your mind sane by exposing it daily to God's word. Keep friends that would help you develop intimacy with God and discipline what you watch and listen to.

CHAPTER ELEVEN:
BREAKING FREE

"Christ has set us free! This means we are really free. Now hold on to your freedom and don't ever become slaves of the Law again."

- Galatians 5:1(CEV)

The first step to breaking free is the readiness to change. You cannot feel new or different without making a valid change in how you think, speak, act, relate, interact and behave. Suppose you don't reset your thinking faculty, its structures and components. In that case, you will be stuck about how to break free from wrong thinking and a dangerous lifestyle.

Apparently, Jesus Christ give up his life. He made that huge sacrifice for the human race who are bound to the Devil's chains or blindfolded by ignorance. The moment the veil in the temple was torn apart, liberation was given to humanity. As many as receive, the life of Christ receives a new thinking pattern and this is what repentance from dead works is all about. Repentance is not a change of action but a change in mind that directs our actions.

However, not everyone receives the new life that Jesus offered through His death. Jesus was God's provision for humanity to enter into a new life that begins with a new mind. But, some ignore it and choose the old way. Hence, they remain bound by their past pain, the oppression of their sins, and the ignorance of believing that freedom is impossible through Jesus Christ.

The truth is, there would be a time you might feel stuck and helpless, even as a believer. Most times, the reason is that over time, you have stayed with a certain way of thinking and lifestyle. Changing your thinking from the way it is into a new thought pattern will require a lot of deliberate work or discipline. Although it could feel like a difficult task, it is not impossible.

Yes! You might ask if Jesus had delivered me, why do I have to work consciously again for my transformation? I understand that salvation is a free gift of God to humanity through Jesus Christ. Those who receive the gift are saved. Salvation is what happened to your Spirit but not your soul. What your soul needs is repentance. One major component of your soul is your mind, which affects how you think and act.

So, your soul, which is a seat for your mind, is being saved. This means that your soul's transformation is not immediate but progress as you begin to learn a new thought pattern by reading God's word and praying.

Now, you need to understand that your mind's change that brings absolute freedom does not come without a serious contention daily in your thought. This contention for change makes the mind a battlefield. You begin to fight in your mind between wrong and right thoughts, past mistakes and future prospects, good and bad and so on.

Sometimes, it will be as if you are losing the battle of your mind. Everything could feel like nothing is changing. You could perceive that there is more to you than the habit that had to hold you bound, but the pleasure of the habit would still want to keep you there. The problem is not with the habit but the process that led to the habit, which starts as an innocent thought in your mind.

BARRIERS IN THE MIND

"The only limits that exist are the ones in your own mind."

- Anonymous

The battle continues in your mind as you progress to wanting to change. You need to be willing to let go to move forward, but a barrier wants to keep you from changing. Barriers of thoughts are those things or vices that limit and serve as a blockade to expanding human thoughts to think possibility and reality.

These barriers are your imagination of events from the past, which had formed a major part of your life. They are the limiting power of change in your mind, which must be dealt with if you want to be absolutely free. It is contained in a person's imaginative thoughts that limit hope and possibilities and resist changing. Your true self is lived from your inside. But when you allow your thought to change from what used to hold you bound into who you are supposed to be. These barriers of thoughts include;

110

- ✓ The Turbulent Water of Anxiety
- ✓ The Barrier of Fear
- ✓ The Deep Valley of Low esteem

The Turbulent Water of Anxiety

"Anxiety does not empty tomorrow of its sorrows, but only empties today of its strength."

— Charles Spurgeon

Anxiety is frequent unrest in your mind about something you anticipate but yet to get. Sometimes, you can desire something great and begin to do things that will bring you closer to it. However, if you do not channel your thinking well, you might lose it because anxiety creates a measure of doubt in your mind.

The universe is created in such a way that what you attract your most dominant thoughts, either it is negative or positive. The problem with the barrier of anxiety is that it does not anticipate anything good. An anxious mind is often filled with the negativity of "what ifs."

Anxiety leads to worry and invariably keeps you from the process of changing and becoming free. Worry takes away your peace and keeps you in the pain of your past. Those who worry remain prisoners of their past and this keeps them down as long as they worry. We begin to worry about things we know and do not know, not sure which one to trust. If you truly want to break free, you must shun anxiety that leads to worry. If you desire change, quit worrying over things you cannot change.

The Bible says;

"Be anxious for nothing, but in everything by prayer and supplication, with thanksgiving, let your requests be made known to God."

Philippians 4:6

Amazing! You must understand that anxiety is towards having something or doing something. However, the Bible clearly shows us that if we truly desire a change and be free, the process does not begin with anxiety. It starts with prayers. I have come to learn this major principle in life. You see, when the issues of life become so overwhelming, the best thing to do is not to become worrisome but pray.

Prayers relieve the mind of stress, anxiety and worries. When you pray, you enable your mind to trust God for change. No man can change any man or truly makes another person free except by the power of God. While prayers are an effective tool for transformation, you must also know that there is nothing wrong when seeking counsel from experts. God had also endowed Counsellors with the wisdom to handle life issues, especially emotional issues like anxiety.

The Barrier of Fear

Another barrier in the mind that keeps us from truly free is the barrier of fear. The Bible says;

"For God has not given us a spirit of fear, but of power and of love and of a sound mind."

- 2 Timothy 1:7

Whatever God gives is for us forever and you must know that fear is never God's gift to humanity. If you live in perpetual fear, you need to be free from it today. The way fear operates is that it gives you a false knowledge of what is not real. When you see someone who is fearful, every situation will look like it will take their life.

Fear puts you on the negative side of life. Your mind begins to focus on oppression, death, impossibility and all forms of thought patterns that do not align with your true self. Fear is never part of your make. God made you with a sound mind. Therefore, nothing good you conceive will ever be impossible for you because you have the mind of God. There is nothing to fear because what you call fear itself is an acronym for False Evidence Appearing Real (F.E.A.R).

God wants you and me to always approach any form of a difficult situation with a mind full of faith instead of fear. Does it mean that you will not be confronted with challenges that will make you fearful? No. Daily, as you aspire for a new and beautiful life, there will be challenges that attack your mind and make you think that your situation will remain the same. At those times, you do not keep silent.

Fear thrives more when you allow it fires at your mind negative thoughts continuously without you saying anything. You dispel the grip of fear by your confession of faith. Many people do not understand the potency of words, especially the ones spoken in faith.

Your words of faith nourish your thoughts, while fear is like the unwanted plant that grows where it is not needed. Now, when you see fear creeping into your thoughts, you must not allow it to gain ground before you rebuke it with the word of faith, which is the knowledge of God's word in your heart. Hence, the study of your Bible helps you grow in faith and work wonders on your mind.

The Deep Valley of Low-Self Esteem

"It's not the lack of ability or opportunity that holds you back; it is only a lack of confidence in yourself."

- Richard Monckton Milnes

Wherever confidence is absent, the will for action ceases. Confidence motivates action and action produces the result. In a word, the deep valley of low self-esteem is the absence of confidence. If you do not believe in change for yourself, no one will and nothing will ever change.

I had rightly said that change begins in your mind and whatever you cannot see in your mind will never be evident in your life.

Low self-esteem is a barrier that blocks the mind from seeing the possibility of change. It makes you see others as though they are more important and better than you. Let's take a lesson from the twelve tribes of Israel that were sent out to spy on the land of Canaan. Out of the twelve, only two came back with a positive result Joshua and Caleb. However, the other ten tribes said to themselves;

"There we saw the giants (the descendants of Anak came from the giants); and we were like grasshoppers in our own sight, and so we were in their sight."

- Numbers 13:33

You see, when you begin to look at yourself as though you are not worth anything in life, that is low self-esteem beckoning at you. Never think of yourself as someone who cannot change and be a better version of yourself. Your background or past might have made you withdraw yourself and reduce you to nobody. But God, who can bring a man from the dunghill and make him a king, says to you that He can transform your life and make you free from the prison of low self-esteem.

Low self-esteem will make you feel insecure in everything you do. It puts you in a position of people's approval before you can appreciate yourself. Once no one approves what you are doing, you feel you are doing nothing or not enough. You are a great, created in the image and likeness of God. So, when the devil tries to mess with your confidence, you should always know that God in you, with you and for you.

Often, you do not always have to get it right the first trial. Nobody does. The truth is that God's creation at the beginning is an indication that whatever will be done excellently well is always a work in progress. The book of Genesis 1:2 says;

"In the beginning, God created the heaven and the earth."

Everyone should have thought that was enough. But God did not stop there. What He had in mind was not yet formed. So, He went further and further until God saw that all He made was good (Genesis 1:31). Dear friend, even God demonstrated that the first trial does not have to be perfect. But you must not stop until you see the change you desired. Do not allow low self-esteem to keep you low. It is time to rise above the status quo. It is time to get out of that pit of insecurity, mediocrity and self-limitation into the total freedom God had provided for us through Jesus Christ.

As mentioned above, the barriers in mind have a way of limiting an individual who desires to be absolutely free. If you want to play safe, then you are not truly ready to be free. Freedom is not a gift. You earn it. The devil does not want anyone to be truly free. He brings all forms of an emotional issue to traumatize you and damp your soul.

TRULY FREE

The devil knows that if he can get access to your mind, he will control your life. So, the point of attack is always the mind. But the good news is, God had brought this book to you as a tool of deliverance to bring you out of the shackles of the devil and deliver absolute freedom to you.

Look, the feeling of being stuck can be likened to quicksand. The more you fight to get out of it, the more you seem to sink in deep. To get out of a quicksand doesn't require an effortless struggle. It requires calmness, strategy and proper planning. Likewise, to be truly free, you need to be calm in your soul and identify what was wrong and how to make the wrong right.

Freedom comes from God and not man. No human can make you truly free. The Bible says,

"Therefore, if the Son makes you free, you shall be free indeed."

- John 8:36

A clear understanding of this scripture shows that true freedom is in God through Christ Jesus. Assuredly, Jesus makes free, but your obligation is not to go back to what had once caused you to be bound. Often, people get imprisoned by habits that start as a thought in their hearts. The more the water the thought, it grows to become an action.

Actions do not lead to habits without some level of consistency. The moment you express your thoughts through action, you give yourself the possibility to continue in that action. This is how bad habits are formed. For instance, a pornography addict wants to be free. Still, most times, He cannot help himself because the act of seeing nude pictures over the internet had already become a habit such that even after salvation, the habit remains.

An addict cannot help himself alone. You need the help of God to bring you out of the situation, not without changing some subtle or seemingly harmless movies you still watch. There are television shows, movies, musicals and auditions that are harmless but constant exposure to them can trigger your need to satisfy your sexual pleasure. Therefore, you need reprogramming in your mind to be free from such a craving for nudity.

Replace those shows with a new set of television programs that edify your soul, make you experience God deeper and refocus your attention to your purpose in life. Habit most times are not eradicated but replaced by redirecting your attention from fueling such habit into something more meaningful to your life. This is how you will truly experience change and be free. It applies to all other aspects of your life where you desire to change.

CHANGING YOURSELF

Nothing will change until you change. Change begins with you. It starts from the first action you take after realizing the need to do better, be better, and offer better in life, ministry, and family. When life throws you lemons, don't relent and give up or the run-up to a corner and cry your eyes out. Retaliate! Make lemonade out of the bitter lemons. This means that there is no situation too difficult that you cannot turn around for your good. All you need is the right attitude and perspective about the situation. Remember, all things work together for your good and not against you.

My advice to you is that you should not be the jailer of your own prison. Be careful about your choices and decision in life. It is easy to make a wrong choice when you have heightened emotions and very much easier to make a bad decision when you are angry. So, when you are at any of these two extremes, it is wise to remain silent so that you do not trap your life by your words.

Consequently, You would be surprised to know how much people cage themselves around their circumstances without the foreknowledge that there is a need to be different from the rest or be better than what people in that same circumstances have been. It is shocking when you hear people say, "In my community, nobody ever goes past a certain level, or in my family, we get to the point of struggle and stop." Now, ask yourself, what is so wrong with stretching far and going beyond? What crime is there in breaking free from every limitation that has been set for you unconsciously or deliberately?

In an actual sense, the fear of the unknown creates enough reasons not to make a change for what you want. Then, you begin to think of the 'if' in negativity. You see, the Devil is so sly that he would manipulate you to see no positive ends to wanting to break free. The only thoughts that would fill your heart would be on the wrong side. But, you have to shake them off so that you do not be a prisoner of your own thoughts, thereby making you a puppet to the devil.

Stop setting bondages and limitations for yourself. Set off to break free. It is an ugly and terrifying feeling to be stuck about what next in your life. There are thousands of people out there experiencing this right now. Self-limiting thought becomes more terrifying because it does not just limit you and hold you down, but it also has some danger attached to it. A few of these dangers will be discussed below;

Losing oneself

A major danger of self-limiting thought is the tendency to lose yourself. Self-limiting is most evident when you try to measure yourself with someone else or by what the person does. You do not know that comparing yourself to someone is limiting yourself to how far the person can go in life.

Self-limiting thoughts put you at the mercy of others. Both their mistakes and errors would eventually become your lifestyle because you have not learned how you can become a better version of yourself rather than measure up with someone else.

The truth is, self-limiting thought makes you rapidly lose your connection to the true essence of life. It can even lead to cutting ties to the people that can truly help you grow and become better. Do not be a prisoner to self-limiting thoughts. You can be more and do more. Aspire for greatness.

Depression

"That's the thing about depression: A human being can survive almost anything, as long as she sees the end in sight. But depression is so insidious, and it compounds daily, that it's impossible to ever see the end."

- Elizabeth Wurtzel

The issue of depression pops up in everything negative. It is just there, lurking around and ready to overcome anybody that gives themselves to it. Depression steals the joy of your soul. It feeds on everything that makes you happy. The danger of depression is that it darkens your heart and makes you see the part of your life that seems not too okay.

Many people fall into depression because they find it hard to see anything right about their lives, which is a lie from the pit of hell. The mere fact that you are still alive is an indication of future hope. Do not give room for depression in your mind. It is a joy stealer.

Alternate Reality

Self-limiting thoughts mess with your mental health. It will make you withdraw from the world and allow you to begin to unconsciously create a universe that is wholly different from your reality.

People never want to come out of this stage because they mostly feel a pseudo-achievement and satisfaction with the unreal world they created rather than the true world of beauty and possibility before them. In this situation, facing the truth becomes the hardest thing ever. You would rather lie to yourself than take the reality of the truth to heart. This is one of the prisons people get into and they need to be free from it.

Face your fear and be ready for a change. Whatever challenges you should make you stronger and not imprison you. See challenges as a stepping stone into your next level. However, whatever you cannot handle yourself, speak up to people whom you trust and believe could be of great help to you.

HOW TO BE TRULY FREE FROM THE IMPRISONMENT IN YOUR MIND

If you have been a prisoner to your mind, here are some ways you can be free from the thoughts that had incarcerated you.

1. Bid your past goodbye

Many people are prisoners of their past. You must realize that your past mistakes, choices and decisions could imprison you. Therefore, always let go of your past if you want to truly free to enjoy life. Some people get to realize that the life they live is not what they want for themselves. They realize they could do better if they step out and break free from their past bitterness.

The burden of your past is too heavy a load for the journey into your future. You must learn to travel light in your mind. How? Forgive yourself and forgive others so that your mind will be clear to see where God is taking you.

2. Knowing your motivation for becoming free (associate yourself with the 'why')

The resounding question of why you have to get out of where you find yourself should keep resounding in your mind. Purpose defines your life direction and you cannot know purpose without understanding the 'why' for your creation. Every one of us has a definite reason for our creation. God had embedded these even before we were born.

The why for your creation is the call of God upon your life, which you must fulfill. Nothing else will matter in life until you find what God had ordained you to do in life. The simple way to know about your purpose is to ask your creator. Know what God had made you do and do it well. Find motivation in your purpose and you will enjoy the reason for living.

3. Free your inner man

Within everyone is a burning force that wants to do better than they do. It just wants to show itself approve, please, free that fire. Let it burn; let it do as it ought to. Trust and follow your instincts, don't be controlled by the 'what if's that can come your way, let the burning fire lead the way and you follow suit.

4. Take Actions

It is not just about having the intentions to do something; it is about doing it regardless. Taking charge and acting out on already decided strategies to get out of your limited box. You can force a horse to the river, but you can never make it drink the water. It is all on you and whatever actions that you take. Things will only happen when you take action to make it change, and that should be what every person should know and be ready to take action. Quit waiting for the messiah that would come to drag you out of the pitfall; pull yourself out. Time waits for no man, and so man shouldn't wait for time. Work with the moment you have and make a breakthrough in breaking free.

> *"Live as free people, but do not use your freedom as a cover-up for evil; live as God's slaves."*

- 1 Peter 2:16

Always bear in mind that you're not a person of your own as a Christian that understands the details of God. In God, you have been given full grace and freedom; nothing can hold you back from serving God and living your best life. So, no matter what the Devil has in stock for, you are covered because God is with you no matter the schemes he has prepared.

All that needs to be done is for you to trust God too much to give up and be willing at all times to fight back and break free. Constantly remind yourself of everything you do. There is no limit, and even when there is an obvious blockage or obstacles, don't let it hold you down. You're God's own and He has designed you for so many great things. Hence, the freedom He gave us through Jesus Christ.